THE CRAFT OF COMPOSITION

The Craft of Composition

Activities and Advice for College Writers

Kris Keeney
Normandale Community College

Prentice Hall, Upper Saddle River, New Jersey 07458

Editorial Director: *Charlyce Jones Owens*
Editor in Chief: *Leah Jewell*
Assistant Editor: *Vivian Garcia*
Senior Managing Editor: *Bonnie Biller*
Production Liaison: *Fran Russello*
Project Manager: *Marianne Hutchinson (Pine Tree Composition)*
Prepress and Manufacturing Buyer: *Mary Ann Gloriande*
Cover Director: *Jayne Conte*
Marketing Manager: *Sue Brekka*

The book was set in 10/12 Stone Serif by Pine Tree Composition
and was printed and bound by Courier Companies, Inc.
The cover was printed by Phoenix Color Corp.

Printed in the United States of America

10   9   8   7   6   5   4   3   2   1

ISBN 0-13-080603-X

Prentice-Hall International (UK) Limited, *London*
Prentice-Hall of Australia Pty, Limited, *Sydney*
Prentice-Hall Canada Inc., *Toronto*
Prentice-Hall Hispanoamericana, S.A., *Mexico*
Prentice-Hall of India Private Limited, *New Delhi*
Prentice-Hall of Japan, Inc., *Tokyo*
Pearson Education Asia Pte. Ltd., *Singapore*
Editora Prentice-Hall do Brasil, Ltda., *Rio de Janeiro*

Contents

3   The Evaluative/Interpretive Essay   51

4   The Argument/Research Essay   69

Preface

To the Student

English composition is a required course in almost every institution of higher learning. At most institutions, this course fulfills several purposes: including:

- Improving students' communication skills
- Preparing students to write better essays and papers for other college courses
- Preparing students to write and communicate more effectively in the workplace
- Improving students' critical thinking skills

This textbook was designed to fulfill the above purposes, among others.

Usually there is a large variety in the interests and abilities of students in a composition class. Some may be English majors, who are confident in their writing abilities; some may dread English, and be quite pessimistic about their chances of success. Whatever your background in the subject, you have the potential to become a better writer, because writing is a skill that can be learned.

Since writing is a skill, the only way to improve your writing is to practice the craft of writing. The guided assignments and activities in this textbook will help you exercise the writing and thinking skills necessary to a good essay. All of the activities in this book have been successfully classroom-tested by students like yourself. In fact, most of the activities in this book were originally designed to answer questions asked by students, or to address problems students were encountering in the writing of an essay. The web sites listed in the back of the book can also be quite useful.

Every day, we use writing to express ourselves, to connect with others, to inform others, to make a point. The rewards of improving your writing are many, including: improved relationships with others; improved grades, and increased chances of promotion at work. It is my hope that in addition to fulfilling the basic purposes of a communication course, this book will help you become a better writer and a better communicator.

Kris Keeney

Acknowledgments

The process of writing, revising, organizing, and publishing a textbook requires the input and assistance of many people. None of the material in this text would have been generated if not for the questions and concerns of my students during the past nine years. To all of my former students at Minnesota State University, Bainbridge College, and Des Moines Area Community College, and to my current students at Normandale Community College, I say a big thank you. I would especially like to thank the students who contributed their own essays to this textbook: Michael Tearney, Genese Dominick, Julie Freeman, Shruthi Manjunath, and Michael Badeaux.

I also owe a large debt of thanks to my reviewers: Thomas J. Giannotti, Jr. of California State University–Dominguez Hills; Anne O'Meara, of Minnesota State University, Mankato; Jennifer Driscoll, of the University of Wisconsin-Milwaukee; Dr. Pamela Howell, Midland College; Dr. Lois Gordon, Fairleigh Dickinson University; and Sister Elizabeth Michael, O.P. Caldwell College. Their thoughtful, professional comments greatly assisted me in the revision of this text.

This text never would have been published if not for the gentle goading of my Prentice-Hall sales representative, Jeffrey Krumm, who somehow knew I had a book inside my head. Thanks are also due to the infinitely patient and encouraging editorial staff at Prentice Hall, especially Vivian Garcia and Leah Jewell.

I would also like to express appreciation to the members of my local writing group: Nancy Goheen, Karin Wiberg, Carolyn Beatty, and Julia Bardwell. They believed in this project from the beginning, and have consistently provided me with excellent editorial advice.

Most of all, I would like to thank my husband, Rick Keeney. Since 1987, when we met in a writing class, I have admired his creativity and talent for editing. His understanding, devotion and sense of humor made the task of writing this textbook much more gratifying.

1

The Narrative Essay

Narrative Essay Overview

The first writing you ever experienced was probably written in the form of a story. Every culture in the world depends upon storytelling to relay its history to younger generations. If you think about it, you can probably remember some classic family stories that are repeated occasionally when your whole family gets together. People tell stories to make sense of their own personal history, to teach others about the joys and sorrows of being human, and to make connections with others.

A narrative essay is most often written in the first person, from the "I, me, my" point of view. The main character of the essay is the narrator. The essay gives you a chance to share an experience of yours with your instructor and the class.

Studying the Narrative Essay

Read the following student examples of narrative essays, and answer the questions that follow each one. While you read, think about what makes this type of essay different from other types of writing. What keeps you interested in the story? What questions come to mind as you read? One effective way to record your reactions is to write notes to yourself in the margins; or you may want to keep a reading journal in which you write your reactions.

A Lesson on the Ice
Mike Tearney

I sat and stared across the barren ice. It had a unique beauty and peace to it. The sunshine made the ice sparkle like thousands of tiny stars. A few lonely leaves danced in a beautiful ballet, as the wind whisked across the crystal floor. The cold air hit my neck and sent a chill down my back. It was a refreshing sensation, like standing out in an early April morning rain. I reached down and picked up a handful of snow. The fine powder swirled away as I threw it out of my hand. I looked out through it and imagined I was in one of those tiny snow domes looking out. A break from reality was what I needed right now.

My mind was still in turmoil over the morning artillery barrage. My thoughts were completely cluttered. It had been one thing after another. I had worked overtime the night before, even though I'd promised not to. Then my girlfriend Chris and I had one of our biggest arguments yet. I wasn't in the mood for anything that morning, so when the fight started, I retreated. I decided to go ice fishing. I couldn't seem to escape, though. Her voice kept ringing over and over in my head.

***

"You said you were getting off early last night! I can't plan anything around you. You're just so selfish. Here's breakfast; it's your supper you didn't come home for!" Chris screamed as she threw down some leftover meatloaf.

"I'm sorry; it wasn't my idea to work a twelve-hour shift. I'd like some time off, too."

"What's that supposed to mean—*too?* Are you saying I don't do my share?"

"No, that's not what I meant."

"Bull! So what's Connie up to these days?" Chris's face was red. She always brought up my ex-girlfriend, who was also my boss at work.

"Get off it! Leave me alone." My head started to ache.

***

My mind tried to focus back on the lake. I took a short step towards the frozen expanse, and one of the ice picks in my pockets poked me. I looked down and then back at the lake; it seemed to have a duller look. The ice wasn't nearly as inviting. It was light gray in spots. I remembered the saying, "Black and white are nice, but don't trust gray." I thought to myself, "It looks safe enough; what the heck? What else could go wrong? Besides, my favorite spot's open. I'll be fine. I'm not going back to the house and listen to her bitch." I grabbed my gear and started out onto the ice.

The ice seemed to make strange sounds as I walked, though it didn't really bother me. Maybe I just didn't care. I was too distracted by the way the day had started. My thoughts drifted back to the fight.

***

"Get off it? I haven't started yet!" Chris screamed and began to cry.

"I said I'm sorry, but that's not good enough anymore. You always bring the Connie thing up. You're so insecure. She's my boss. I can't blink without you bitching. Can't you just give it a break? We need the extra cash."

"Money, money. Is that all that's important anymore? What about us?"

"I don't know. I can't think straight right now. Things just aren't working out. It's been two years; I don't know what to say or do."

Chris bit her lip. "Maybe we should call it quits."

***

Suddenly there was a long "twang" beneath me, as the ice started to crack. I tried to sprawl out, but it was too late. As I started to fall through the ice, my mind was suddenly bashed out of its dreamscape. I was in serious trouble. The water rushed in over the top of me.

The cold hit, and I felt the air rush from my lungs. I pushed my gear away and frantically grabbed for a handhold. Bubbles rushed by and blinded me as I tried to regain my bearings. My mind was encompassed in fear. Only one thought was present now: "I'm going to die."

I felt a numbness start to creep over my mind. Some tiny bit of sanity returned as I looked up and saw a dark spot. Somewhere in my confused state, I remembered hearing that you're supposed to swim to the dark spot. Yes, I knew that's what I had to do if I was going to make it. I pushed off the bottom, and with a couple of breaststrokes I reached the spot. Then, with a strong kick, I pushed myself through the slushy ice and into the open air. I grabbed a much-needed breath. I coughed several times as I tried to regain normal breathing.

I reached for my pocket; thank God they were still there—two ice picks. I grabbed them and started clawing at the ice around me, while I prayed the ice farther out was enough to pull me out of my frozen state. I managed to catch a grip with one pick and then the other. There was no feeling left in my hands, and my body seemed to be a weight, pulling me back into the icy waters. I continued to struggle, bit by bit, until my body lay on top of the ice. I could still hear the ice cracking beneath my weight. I crawled away from the hole toward the shore and safety. It seemed to be an eternity away. When I reached solid ground, I rolled onto my back and looked into the sky. I tried to grasp what had taken place.

How stupid could I be? Why did I even go out on the ice? Then I remembered the argument: ". . . maybe we should call it quits." I almost did. I was completely drained of all energy. I was freezing and totally soaked. Reality had just kicked in and some serious revelations came to me: Am I alive? Is there a God? I've found that many times in the past I've lost my priorities. It doesn't happen all at once. First it's one thing and then another, until I finally lose perspective. The most trivial things become my life's center. Then I'll find I have one crisis after another.

That was the case that winter. My life had become so sterile; I wasn't seeing the whole picture. I was already inside that tiny snow dome.

I learned a lot that day. I won't go out on thin ice because I'm mad or distracted. I found that sometimes I need to step back from a problem and think clearly, then decide what's really important. I don't have to rush into things blindly. My highest priority is life itself. I will live and enjoy it! It's the only one I get.

1. Without looking at the narrative essay above, write for five minutes about the things you remember from the essay. When you've finished, compare your recollections with others in the class. As a class, decide which details, images, and messages were the most memorable.
2. Why did Mike write this essay? What message does he have to share with his audience?
3. Where in the essay does Mike foreshadow the crisis of falling through the ice? Did you guess what was going to happen? How does he make you want to read further?
4. What descriptions in the essay seem the most realistic? Why?
5. Think about your own experiences. Have you ever been in a similar situation? What event in your life most clearly mirrors Mike's experience?
6. Look at this essay with a critical eye. What would you change about it? Why?

Mirror, Mirror
Genese Dominick

Looking in the mirror was something I spent a lot of time doing. I wasn't looking at my face, applying makeup, or doing my hair. I was pinching fat until my skin turned red and blotchy, crying, and trying to find bigger clothes to hide my obesity. Nothing seemed to get rid of my new obsession. At first, I thought being concerned about my fat was just a phase; it was something all normal teenage girls go through. It wasn't until my friends became worried enough to tell my mom exactly how obsessive I'd become that I noticed this wasn't just a phase.

It began when I was thirteen. I was talking to two of my friends about boys and clothes, the usual. My friend Jen had two older brothers who were the objects of all her friends' affections. On that specific day, something Jen told me changed my life forever.

"Hey, Gese, guess what Jay said about you the other day?"

"What?!" Your brother knows I'm alive? Yeah, right. What did he *supposedly* say about me?"

"Well, he thinks you're gonna be hot someday. He just said you need to lose a little weight first. Said you were too chunky. But don't worry. I told him you weren't *that* fat."

"Thanks. Glad you don't think I'm a goddam whale."

The moment I heard those words, it was like a brick crashed down on my shoulders. I could taste the acidy bitterness of bile mixing with my freshly devoured glazed doughnut. See, every day after school we went to the town's bakery for doughnuts and Dr. Pepper. From then on, however, I knew my bakery days had to be over. I couldn't believe Jay thought I was fat, and I never stopped to notice myself.

In those days, I guess I was a little chunky. At 5′5″ and 145 pounds, I was nowhere near the point of starvation. I always blamed my weight on puberty. That, at least was acceptable. It couldn't be that I had lost control of my eating. No way.

"You know, someday all this fat will find the right places to go, and you're gonna regret ever making fun of me," I would say to all the people who felt the need to discuss my body size. Coming from a small town, there were quite a few of them too.

My days became seemingly shorter. After the "bakery incident," I went home and looked in magazines for models who had bodies like the one I suddenly desired. I would pull out page after page of heavier models and put thinner models underneath them until I got to the thinnest model I had seen yet. I made a type of calendar, and as the weight came off, the picture did too. My goals were reached this way, although I became too sick and weak to make it to my final goal.

When I lost my first ten pounds, I noticed guys would look my way more often; friends would comment on how good I was looking. This did nothing to help my situation, obviously. The more people commented on my weight, the more frustrated I became. Didn't people see who I was on the inside?

I started to wear baggier clothes to cover my shrinking body. The more concerned with appearances people became, the larger my clothes became. I wanted to have people like me for who I was on the inside, not for what I looked like on the outside.

Naturally, if I had waked up and taken a good look at myself, I would have realized my friends weren't my friends because of my body—it was absolutely disgusting. I weighed 103 pounds at 5'8". I was tired all the time, with huge black circles under my sunken eyes. I could count every single bone in my body; they protruded from me like chicken wings. Every time I stood up, my legs would wobble, and I would black out.

I'm not going to discuss the methods I used to lose all the weight. Some of them are too disgusting to mention, and some of them are things I still cannot reflect on without feeling ill. Anorexia is serious, and the people who have it actually want help but don't know how to find it.

One day, in my health class, we were watching a film about an anorexic girl. She reminded me so much of myself, and I still wonder if my teacher showed it to our class at that time for a specific reason. See, anorexia didn't have anything to do with what we were discussing in class at that time. Anyway, the girl in the movie had to be put into a hospital. They inserted tubes in various parts of her body to keep her alive. When they told her she might have to have a tube stuck in her chest bone if she continued to lose weight, I felt like the doctors were talking to me. I began sweating and got very cold, almost like I was anticipating it myself. The feelings were scary, and I remember some of my classmates looking at me a bit funny. My pencil dropped on the floor, and the last thing I remember is hearing the lead break on the cement. That snapping sound was echoing in my head when I woke up about five minutes later with two teachers peering down at me.

Fainting is what turned a new leaf on the whole dieting issue. My mom came to the school from work and was crying. Some of my teachers were crying too. I went to a hospital in Des Moines to get treatment shortly after that incident. I was scared I would hurt someone else if I fainted while driving or something would cause pain to someone I loved. I still didn't care what would happen to me; I had lost control, something I hated losing.

The first trip to the hospital was futile, for the most part. I didn't care what they said would happen to me. A fat lady was my counselor; what did she know about losing weight? She was probably just jealous she couldn't do whatever I was doing. I held a power over her. She told me I would lose my hair and my teeth would fall out. Naturally, I thought she was full of it. Who cares? As long as I don't get fat, my whole body could fall to pieces. I sat there with a pissed off look on my face and took what she dished out.

We got home and my mom made this huge supper, I remember. I couldn't eat much because it would make me sick. One of the benefits of such long-term starvation was that I couldn't eat much even if I wanted to. Trying to tell this to my mom was impossible. For the next three weeks, she watched me like a hawk, and when I was still losing weight, she set me up for another appointment.

I wasn't as opposed to going back this time. I was tired of how I was living. I began to want help. I think my mom noticed that little fact be-cause I would drop hints every now and then. For instance, I would complain about how bad I was feeling, something I never did before, or casually let her get a glimpse of my emaciated body. I was ready to be normal; the time was now or never.

I got help again, but I cannot say I was completely cured. When I eat, I still look at fat content and do a few other silly rituals I never could stop. If I stopped, I would have lost total control. I still compare my body to thinner ones and hate the fact that mine is so much bigger. I notice when things don't go as *I* planned, I tend to lose weight easily. I hated following the diet they gave me to follow, but at least I never had to have a tube my chest bone. Someday, I hope to put all of this behind me. I'm looking forward to that day.

1. State the main idea of this essay in one sentence. Is this difficult to do? Why or why not?
2. What societal issue(s) does this essay address?
3. What about Genese's essay makes it realistic or easy to believe?
4. Do you feel as if this story is resolved? Why or why not?
5. What details/descriptions in the essay are the most effective or memorable? Why?
6. Look at this essay with a critical eye. What would you change about it? Why?

The Narrative Essay in Everyday Life

Finishing the Story

In order to write an interesting narrative, you must first understand the structure of a good story. You probably subconsciously understand this structure because you have been hearing stories your whole life. But as you are completing the following activity, think about what's going on. Why are you writing the details you are writing?

Read the following story, and then write an ending.

T. J. walked down the deserted downtown street. It was quiet; too quiet. Dark shadows from the buildings around him signalled that the sun was setting quickly. T. J. shivered and pulled his thin jean jacket around his shoulders; he carefully pulled his Mariner's hat over his ears so that it wouldn't blow off.

Over the sound of cars whizzing by on the nearby freeway, T. J. could hear the sirens wailing. The sound grew louder and louder, closer and closer. He grasped the knife he held in his pocket and turned his head from side to side, listening.

"I can't believe I came here. How dumb can I be?" T. J. thought to himself, picking up his pace. The bridge was only about half a mile away, and then he would be all right.

T. J. heard footsteps running behind him; the sirens were getting closer and closer. He grasped the knife and whirled around.

Questions for Discussion

1. Which parts of the story build suspense?
2. What questions did you have after reading the first half of the story? What conflicts needed to be resolved?
3. Get into groups of three or four and discuss how you resolved the conflicts in this story. Comment on what you enjoyed about your group members' versions of the end of the story.

Writing Dialogue

There are three rules for writing good dialogue:

1. Use correct punctuation and paragraphing.

In dialogue, quotation marks belong at the beginning and the end of the words a character speaks. All punctuation goes inside the quotation marks.

Example:
    Ineffective: "Mary, come over here! Mike yelled."

    More Effective: "Mary, come over here!" Mike yelled.

When writing dialogue, begin a new paragraph each time a new person speaks or reacts nonverbally to the other speaker(s).

Example:

Ineffective: "I didn't spill the coffee," Mary sniffed. "I saw you do it, so don't lie," Mike snarled. "You're cleaning up that mess right now."

More Effective: "I didn't spill the coffee," Mary sniffed.
"I saw you do it, so don't lie," Mike snarled. "You're cleaning up that mess right now."

2. Show, don't tell, how characters feel or react, and avoid speech tags.
Avoid using adverbs to describe voice qualities or emotions of a speaker (words like lovingly, sadly, etc.). It is much more effective to describe a speaker's facial expression instead (smiling, frowning, etc.). Speech tags (he said, she replied, etc.) are also unnecessary most of the time, because the new paragraphs indicate when the speakers change.

Example:

Ineffective: You're so sweet," Jane said lovingly.
"But you said you wouldn't go to the prom with me," Jack said sadly.

More Effective: "You're so sweet." Jane smiled and ran her fingers through Jack's hair.
"But you said you wouldn't go to the prom with me." Jack stared at the sidewalk and shuffled his feet.

3. Use "real" language.
Avoid stilted, formal language. Very few people speak in a grammatically correct manner; don't write dialogue that doesn't sound like your characters.

Example:

Ineffective: "I love you wholeheartedly, John. No one will ever take your place in my heart." Sally looked deep into John's eyes, which were filling with tears.
"Sally, you are my life. Will you marry me?" John swept Sally into a passionate embrace.

More Effective: "Hey, John, if ya love me you'll get up off the couch and grab me another beer." Sally shoved John off of the battered sofa and onto the floor.
"Yeah, well, if I buy ya that ring you'll have to start gettin' yer own beer, honey." John lumbered to the kitchen and opened the refrigerator.

"Eavesdropping" on Dialogue

Go to a busy area of campus: a cafeteria, a common area, a recreation room. Try to find some people talking, and sit near enough to them so you can hear their conversation without being obvious. Pretending to study usually works. Write down what they say to one another, as closely as you can (you may have to develop a kind of shorthand to get this accomplished!). After a few minutes, leave, go directly to a computer, and type the conversation. Don't identify the people; just briefly describe their looks, their mannerisms, and of course, recreate their dialogue. Bring your results to the next class meeting. Then get into small groups and do the following:

1. Have everyone in the group read his or her dialogue aloud. As this is being done, feel free to comment on the dialogue, noting how the writer has incorporated body language, expressions, and so on.

2. Pass your dialogue sheet to someone else in the group. Look at your partner's dialogue. Is it written correctly, using the right paragraphing and punctuation? If not, mark the errors.

3. As a group, discuss what makes good dialogue. Whose dialogue was the funniest? the most realistic? What methods did this person use to write good dialogue?

Variation of the "Eavesdropping" Activity   Watch a television show agreed on by the class, and try to write down five minutes of conversation as you hear it said (it usually works best to tape the show, so you can watch the dialogue a few times). Add body language, descriptions of the characters, and so forth. When you have finished, get into small groups and compare your answers. What details did you notice that others didn't? What details did you miss? Who recreated the conversation most realistically? What methods did this person use to write good dialogue?

Sensory Description

In order to make a moment come alive for the reader, a writer must strive to *show,* not tell, what is happening. In our daily lives, we are very used to "telling" people stories, not "showing" people what happened. In writing, however, it is much easier to interest the reader if vivid, sensory description is employed. Most people are good at writing that uses only one of the five senses—sight. But really vivid writing uses all the senses—hearing, smell, touch/feeling, taste, *and* sight. Read the following examples, and then discuss the questions that follow.

Boring: I pulled the car to the starting line. Keith stood in front of me and held up an old rag. I checked the gauges and got ready for him to signal the start of the race.

Interesting: I revved the engine up a couple of times and let the clutch pop so the tires could warm up a bit against the cool cement of the drag strip. Keith walked out in front of the starting line about 20 feet. I pulled up to the starting line until someone signaled that the nose of Betsymay, the name for my Chevelle, was even with the fading line. Keith raised his arms with a red shop rag in his hands. I pushed my right foot down until the engine came to a screaming roar. My left foot shook from pushing in the clutch pedal on the Zoom racing clutch plates. The rpms of the engine continued to climb until they reached 5500. The car shook, the smell of gasoline was on the edge of being detected, and the thundering of the dual exhausts rang in my ears. The ringing would last long after the race was finished. (Glenn Atwell, "Top Gun"—originally published in the *Skunk River Review* 1995)

1. What images are the most memorable? Why?
2. What does the fact that Glenn named his car tell the reader about Glenn? Why did he include this information?
3. Why did Glenn use so many sound images?

Description   There are two main types of description: Straight description and simile/metaphor. Try to use both in your essay.

Straight Description   Straight Description is simply describing a person, place, thing, or scene in a way that makes the reader see what is going on. Try to use as many sensory words as possible when you use straight description (sight, sound, smell, taste, and touch words).

Example:

1. *The umbrella was by the bench.*

1. The wet, pink-and-purple-striped umbrella lay crumpled next to the wooden park bench.

2. *The woman sang to me.*

2. The large, 40-ish woman, smelling of lavender and dripping sweat, put her chubby hand on my shoulder and sang "Danny Boy" in an off-key voice.

Try the following on your own, and then read your answers to the class.

1. *The boy dropped his treat.*
2. *The man motioned me over to the counter.*
3. *The woman offered me soup.*

Simile/Metaphor   When we use simile and metaphor, we use familiar things to describe unfamiliar things. For example, when someone tells you that frog legs taste like chicken, he or she is describing something unfamiliar (frog legs) in terms of the familiar (chicken).

Similes use the word "like" or "as" to compare the unfamiliar to the familiar. For example, the phrase "the ice was smooth as a mirror" could be used to explain how slick the ice was.

Metaphor is a comparison that doesn't use the word "like" or "as." To use the example above and make it a metaphor, we say, "the ice was a slick mirror." Now we know the ice wasn't *actually* a slick mirror, but the metaphor is a poetic way of achieving the same effect as a simile.

When using simile and metaphor, avoid tired, used-up clichés, such as "big as a house" and "white as snow." Try to think up new and interesting similes and metaphors.

For practice, do the following exercises and read your answers to the class:

1. His eyes were flat, like a/an _____.

2. The snow flew around us like _____.

3. The clouds were _____.

4. My heart felt like_____.

Review Activity   Go back to the first section of this chapter, Studying the Narrative, and choose one of the student examples. Then complete the following questions:

1. Put an asterisk (*) next to each place the writer uses all three conditions of good dialogue: correct punctuation and spacing; showing, not telling; and real language.

2. Underline the sections in which the writer uses straight description; circle any similes or metaphors you find.

3. Put checkmarks next to places where the writer could have been more descriptive. Be prepared to explain your marks.

4. Compare your marks to a classmate's, and discuss both the strengths and the weaknesses of the essay. What would you change about it if it were your essay? What would you not change? Why?

Description Activity   Your instructor will give you a piece of fruit. Set it on your desk and look at it. Get out a sheet of paper for making notes and answer the following questions:

1. What does the fruit look like? Describe its color, patterns, shape, and so on. Is it like or unlike others of its species that you have encountered before? How?

2. What does the fruit feel like? Describe its outer texture, comparing it to some animal or object. Cut it apart. How does it feel inside? What do the seeds feel like?

3. Smell the fruit. What other thing does it smell like? What associations do you have with this smell?

4. Cut the fruit again, or think of how it sounded when you cut it. How would you describe that sound, no matter how soft or loud? What kind of noises would you make if you ate the fruit?

5. Taste the fruit. Describe its taste, using both straight description and a comparison to another food.

6. Write down any other sensory words or images you can associate with this fruit.

Discuss your answers in small groups or with the entire class. Write a one-page portrait of your fruit for the next class period.

Soap Opera

We have all watched some kind of serial drama on television. Maybe you watch daytime dramas such as *Days of Our Lives* or *As the World Turns*; perhaps you've watched prime-time serial dramas, such as *Party of Five* or *Babylon 5*. In any case, the idea is the same: We watch familiar characters get into and out of scrapes; we get to know the personalities of the characters as time goes on; and we watch these characters change and grow.

Another aspect of soap operas is the idea of cliché. Many soap operas rely on plot twists or story effects that are old and tired. For example, in the middle of a highly dramatic series of episodes, a character suddenly "wakes up" and the whole series of events turns out to have been a dream (similar to the plot of Lewis Carroll's *Alice in Wonderland*).

Another convention of soap operas is the predictable relationship diffi-
culties of most soap opera couples; after all, if no characters had any
problems, there wouldn't be any plot, would there?

What if you could write your own soap opera? How would you create the tension and suspense necessary to maintain your readers' interest? How would you avoid the cliché events that most soap operas rely
upon?

Here is a cast of characters and an episode from one class's soap
opera. Read the following cast of characters and sample scenes from our
imaginary "soap opera." Then complete the activity as assigned by your
instructor.

Ankeny Place

Cast of Characters:

Karl Weber: Age: 20
>Hair: blond
>Eyes: blue
>Height: 6'
>Weight: 200 lbs.
>Race: Caucasian

Karl grew up on a farm near Waterloo, Iowa. He has never lived near a

city as large as Des Moines. Karl is quiet but very emotional. He misses

his family. Major: Ag Business

Rosanna Wilton: Age: 29
>Hair: dark brown
>Eyes: brown
>Height: 5' 7"
>Weight: 130 lbs.
>Race: African-American

Rosanna is from Des Moines, but she moved to Ankeny after her divorce.

She has two children, but only Matt, her five-year-old, lives with her. Her

seven-year-old boy, Mike, lives with his father in West Des Moines.

Rosanna is very wild and loves to party. She lives next door to Karl.

Major: Nursing

Pete Fleur: Age: 24
>Hair: black

Eyes: brown
Height: 5′ 8″
Weight: 150 lbs.
Race: Native American

Pete grew up on an Indian reservation in North Dakota. He is very quiet and mysterious, and spends a lot of time alone. He has a crush on Noelle, who sits next to him in Composition 1. Major: Liberal Arts

Noelle Broussard: Age: 22
Hair: auburn
Eyes: blue
Height: 5′ 6″
Weight: 130 lbs.
Race: Caucasian

Noelle attended private Catholic girls' schools as a youngster, and she married right after high school. Her husband decided to become a monk, so they divorced two years ago. She baby-sits for Rosanna much of the time, and she secretly has a crush on Karl. Major: Nursing

Rick Johnson: Age: 29
Hair: dark brown
Eyes: brown
Height: 6′ 2″
Weight: 200 lbs.
Race: African-American

Rick is Rosanna's twin brother. He owns Rick's Rockhouse, a local bar and pool hall. He's married to Wendy, and they both work in the bar most of the time. Rick is very friendly and is known as the town gossip, getting most of the news from his customers. Major: Business

Wendy Johnson: Age: 21
Hair: blond
Eyes: brown
Height: 5′ 2″
Weight: 110 lbs.
Race: Caucasian

Wendy is Rick's wife and Noelle's first cousin. She was a Harley-Davidson devotee for two years before she "settled down" and married Rick. Wendy is six months pregnant. Major: Accounting

Maria Wilton: Age: 55
> Hair: silver
> Eyes: brown
> Height: 5' 5"
> Weight: 115 lbs.
> Race: Caucasian, Hispanic descent

Maria is Rosanna's ex-mother-in-law. She is trying to gain custody of both grandchildren. She recently secretly bought Ankeny Place and regularly goes there to spy on Rosanna.

Stuart Wilton: Age: 35
> Hair: black
> Eyes: brown
> Height: 5' 11"
> Weight: 175 lbs.
> Race: Caucasian

Stuart is Maria's son and Rosanna's ex-husband. He wants Rosanna back and has no idea about his mother's plot to gain custody of their children. He lost his job four months ago and is taking auto mechanic classes.

Trent Herman: Age: 45
> Hair: brown
> Eyes: blue
> Height: 5' 10"
> Weight: 180 lbs.
> Race: Caucasian

Trent is the building manager for Ankeny Place. He is very friendly with all the tenants, and everyone likes him. He's very interested in Maria. He teaches tennis lessons.

Scene 1: Ankeny Place, Rick and Wendy Johnson's apartment

"I'll be in later tonight, honey." Wendy hugged her husband as she opened the door for him.

"God, it's just work, work, work, every day," Rick moaned.

"Cheer up, put on a happy face. We've gotta save some dough before junior comes around." Wendy swatted Rick on the behind and ushered him out the door.

Just as she was sitting down at the kitchen table to do her accounting homework, the phone rang.

"Hello?"

"Wendy. Shut up and listen to me. I'm coming to get you and my baby. Soon. Be ready." The phone receiver went dead.

Wendy stood completely still, telephone receiver still in her hand. Then she began to shake uncontrollably, and tears ran down her face. She quickly dialed Noelle's number.

"Hi. This is Noelle. I'm really sorry I missed your call, so please leave your name and number, and I'll call you back."

"Noelle! It's Wendy! He's back!" Wendy dissolved into sobs and hung up the phone.

Scene 2: Rick's Rockhouse

"Go ahead and go home, Wanda," Rick yelled across the bar to the waitress on duty.

"See ya, Rick." She whipped off her apron and headed out the door. "You need some quarters in the register."

"Thanks." Rick reached under the bar for a roll of quarters.

"Can I get two Genuine Drafts?" Pete Fleur leaned across the bar. He wore skin-tight blue jeans and a cowboy hat.

"Sure. And if you're Dwight Yoakam, you can sign your napkin and get 'em for free."

"Funny." Pete didn't laugh. "Give me two dollars in quarters, too."

Rick looked across the smoky room to the pool tables. Sure enough, there was his sister Rosanna in a skimpy tank top, staring at Pete's backside.

"Hey, buddy. A word of advice. Don't bet on any game you play with her."

"Oh yeah?" Pete put the quarters in his pocket. "Who are you, her dad?"

"No, I'm her brother." Rick stared at Pete's eyes, barely visible under the cowboy hat.

"Oh. Well, thanks, man." Pete shook his head as he delivered Rosanna's beer.

The door slammed behind Trent Herman. He strode to the bar, taking off his Northrup hat.

"Pour me a tall one, barkeep." Trent wiped his brow.

"Hey Trent, been givin' some tennis lessons today?"

"Hell, no. That sassy new manager's been runnin' me ragged, installing air conditioners, ceiling fans, dishwashers, you name it."

"We're getting that stuff in our apartments?" Rick was worried. Rents would definitely skyrocket if that happened.

"Nope. This stuff is all in her apartment." Trent smiled. "But I don't mind. She's pretty cute. Got some personality. It's been awhile since I met a gal with personality."

"That's cool, Trent. When are you making your move?" Rick chuckled.

"Not for a little while. Gotta warm her up, if you know what I mean."

Both men laughed.

Rosanna walked behind the bar and grabbed Rick's arm. "What the hell did you tell that boy about me?"

"Take it easy, Zan. Nothing."

"He wants to bet $100 on our next game; who the hell is he?"

"I don't know, Zan. I think he moved in next to Karl last week."

"Well, I'm not taking his money away if I have to live two doors down from him."

"Zan, what's wrong? You're feeling sorry for someone?" Rick shook his finger. "You'll never get anywhere with that attitude."

"He gives me the creeps." Rosanna lit a cigarette and poured herself a shot of Cuervo. "But you're right. Since when have I let that get in the way?" Rosanna walked back to the pool table and began racking the balls for a new game.

The door opened again. The man stood still for a moment, to let his eyes focus. He turned toward the pool tables, where Rosanna was sitting on Pete's knee, laughing.

"Get away from my wife, kid!" Stuart charged towards them, fists clenched.

Scene 3: Ankeny Place, Rosanna's apartment

"Good night, sleepyhead." Noelle tucked Matt in. "Have you said your prayers?"

"God Bless Mommy, Daddy, Gamma, and Noelle." Matt stared up at Noelle. "I got a secret. You promise not to tell?"

"I promise." Noelle smiled. "What is it?"

"Gamma told me that we're going on a vacation. We're going to see Mickey Mouse."

"Sure you are." Noelle patted his hand. "Why is that a secret?"

"Because Gamma told me not to tell."

Noelle smiled to herself. Matt hadn't seen his grandma for a month. And she knew Rosanna would never allow Maria to take Matt to Disneyland.

"Well, next time you see her, you ask her when you're going."

"Okay." Matt closed his eyes.

Noelle walked into the living room and picked up a romance novel. Just as she was finishing the first chapter, the phone rang.

"Hi, Rosanna?"

"No, this is Noelle."

"Oh, hi. This is Karl, across the hall."

"Hi." Noelle's heart began to race. She wondered if he could hear it in her voice.

"I'm just calling because when I came in from my car, this person was shining a flashlight into one of the bedroom windows. You want me to come over?"

"Sure. I mean, would you mind?" Noelle hung up the phone and rushed to Matt's room. She cracked open the door. A beam of light danced around on the wall. Noelle crept to the kitchen window, leaving the lights off. As she peered over the window sill, she saw a slight figure turn out the flashlight and creep through the shrubbery.

Karl knocked on the door and walked in quickly, baseball bat in hand. "Did you see who it was?"

Soap Opera Activities

1. Form groups of four or five. Use the characters above, or come up with your own cast of characters. Then assign each group member a different date to continue the soap opera. For example, Student A will write a continuation of each of the original three scenes and then "cliff-hang" the reader. Then Student B will pick up where Student A left off, and so on, until each group member has had a chance to write. The group will get together and write the "ending" together.

2. A variation of the above activity is to keep a journal that continues the soap opera. Each week you can write what's happening in the characters' lives and practice your writing skills at the same time.

Starting Your Narrative Essay

Most people don't just sit down and begin writing a narrative. In fact, it's usually not a good idea to write about the first thing that pops into your head. Often, an idea needs time to grow. Most writers agree that a great way to get started is to pre-write. Pre-writing is any activity that generates ideas; here are some examples of common pre-writing techniques:

Freewriting

You're probably familiar with freewriting from previous courses. Many students prefer a timed, focused freewrite to help them begin. To do this type of freewrite, choose a topic from the list at the end of this section; then write or type whatever comes into your head regarding that topic for a set period of time—five minutes, ten minutes, fifteen minutes—as long you want to spend generating ideas.

Brainstorming

Brainstorming is a cousin of freewriting. Instead of writing one long paragraph, though, a brainstorm is more of a "laundry list" of possibilities. If you tend to think faster than you write, try brainstorming; it's a great way to get all those ideas down on paper quickly.

Clustering

Clustering is a more "artistic" way to generate ideas. To cluster, you need a blank piece of paper. In the middle, write a starting point and circle it (one of the topics below would work well). When a related idea comes to mind, write it on the page, circle it, and connect it to the main topic with a line. If a "sub-idea" of an idea comes to mind, circle it and connect it to the idea. Many times students find that an idea is related to two ideas on the page; fine—connect it to both.

There are many other forms of pre-writing, and your instructor may share some of them with you. Try them all until you find one that works best for you.

Journaling

Another common prewriting activity is journaling. This activity is ongoing; in other words, in order for journaling to work, you must make a commitment to journaling on a regular basis. Once a day is usually best.

There are many different types of journals. Some people keep journals of their everyday activities and their hopes and dreams. Others keep journals for classes, writing down key ideas they find in their reading, recopying notes, and so forth. Some instructors will assign a journal as a class requirement.

If you are journaling to find a topic for your narrative, try writing entries on these topics:

- My most memorable argument or fight and what I learned from it
- A time I was dishonest
- A trick or joke I played on someone else (or a trick or joke that was played on me)
- My most memorable time with my family
- The most outrageous thing I ever did

Topic Possibilities

Here are some other possible topics for your narrative essay. Remember that it is often easier to write a narrative that details an event that happens in a day or less, and the main character must be *you* (that means no topics like "the day my brother broke his leg"—although "the day I broke my leg" would be okay).

1. My most frightening moment
2. The moment I most frightened other people
3. The happiest moment of my life
4. The most wonderful thing I ever did for someone
5. My most embarrassing moment
6. The time I most embarrassed someone else
7. The most memorable lesson I learned at school
8. The most memorable lesson I taught someone else
9. A moment that exceeded my expectations
10. A moment that didn't meet my expectations
11. The meanest thing I ever did to someone
12. My closest brush with death
13. My closest brush with marriage or divorce

14. The achievement I'm most proud of
15. My most memorable illness or injury
16. The most memorable moment on vacation
17. My most memorable victory
18. My brush with the law
19. My memorable moment in the judicial system
20. My most memorable date

Flashbacks

As mentioned before, effective narratives often consist of relating an experience that happens in a day or less. Many students resist this assignment because they feel the need to include information about events that preceded the story in the narrative. This information is easy to incorporate, however, through the use of flashbacks. The student essay earlier in the chapter, "A Lesson on the Ice" by Mike Tearney, incorporates flashbacks.

You've probably seen flashbacks in movies and on television. The lights go soft, music begins to play, the picture gets fuzzy, and poof! You're back in the past. In essays, we don't have the option of blurring the picture to give our reader the cue that we're traveling back in time; instead, we use *transitions.*

Here are some possible transition techniques:

- Begin at the end of your story and use flashbacks to explain the chain of events that led to that end.
- If your story has "dead spots" in which little action occurs over a length of time, use these areas for explanatory flashbacks. You can start with phrases such as, "I thought back to . . ." or "My mind wandered, and I thought of . . ." or use time-transition words such as *before, prior to, then, previously, earlier, at one time.*
- Frame your story; start it just before the critical moment and then flash back to the beginning. The conclusion of your story will resolve the suspense and conflict created in your introduction.

Narrative Essay Checklist

Your narrative essay should include the following:

1. ___ Straight Description
2. ___ Simile/Metaphor

3. ___ Dialogue

4. ___ Showing, not telling

Remember, your narrative should detail a life-altering event; ideally, the main action of this event should take place in a day or less. Some students have written essays on a four-minute foot race and included both great sensory description and considerable dialogue (remember, dialogue can be internal—we are constantly talking to ourselves inside our heads). Good luck!

Revising the Narrative Essay

One of the most important parts of the writing process is the revision process. Realistically, almost every student who receives an unsatisfactory grade can trace the source of his or her problem to bad editing and revision decisions. The following section will give you some tips on revising and editing your essay.

Writing the Rough Draft

Tip #1: Generate enough material to revise.

Imagine you are an ice sculptor. You've been asked to carve a huge ice sculpture for a high-society event. You assemble your carving tools and drive over to the hall; but when you arrive, you find that the only ice available is one little ice cube. Obviously, you can't make the kind of sculpture that has been ordered. What are you going to do?

Your composition instructor may ask you the same question if you bring an "ice cube" to class instead of an "ice chunk." In other words, if your instructor assigns a four-page draft and you bring a poorly written one-page draft, you aren't going to get very far in your revision. Neither you nor your instructor has much to carve—that is, to revise. On the other hand, if you bring in a five- or six-page draft, you have room to cut out unnecessary information and to move facts and details around. Your instructor and classmates will have a much better idea of the story you want to tell and will be able to give you more assistance.

Tip #2: Don't Get Bogged Down with Editing Too Soon.

It's important to know the difference between revising and editing. Revision involves cutting out or adding whole paragraphs, or moving text around in the essay. Editing involves catching punctuation, grammar, and other mechanical errors. Don't agonize over every sentence in your first draft; you can worry about editing later. Just get something down on paper. Editing is a very important part of the writing process, but it should occur fairly late in the process, not right away.

Workshopping the Narrative Essay

One of the most important parts of the writing process involves giving and getting feedback. Peer editing, also known as workshopping, allows you to learn what you need to add or delete from your own writing, and it also allows you to help other students fix their writing. By assisting others, you will often learn a lot about how to fix your own work. Use the following peer editing guide to help you workshop others' essays.

Narrative Peer Editing Checklist

1. Is the writer using flashbacks? If so, are the transitions adequate to cue the reader that a change in time or place is occurring? What could the writer do to improve "time flow"?

If the writer is not using flashbacks, are there adequate transitions from one section to the next? What transition words is the writer overusing? ("Then" and "after" are commonly overused.)

2. Identify the characters in the narrative. What do they look like? What motivates them? If you can't find the answers to these questions, notify the writer. Those details are important.

3. Check the dialogue, making sure that punctuation and paragraphing are done correctly. Indicate to the writer when he or she needs to include a facial expression or description of tone of voice to make the moment more "real" or understandable.

4. What is the writer trying to communicate to you, the reader? Write a short interpretation and read it in group discussion; as a writer, notice other people's impressions. Are your readers "getting it," or do you need to add, delete, or expand on certain areas?

5. Think about the "where" of this piece. If the setting is not described, write questions to the writer about the setting that you would like to see answered.

6. Analyze the introduction and conclusion. How is the writer introducing you to the topic? What improvements could be made? How does the conclusion tie up the ends of the story? What could be improved about the conclusion?

7. Choose a good-sized paragraph (three lines or more) and analyze it for forms of the verb "to be" (is, was, were, am, are, etc.). Suggest stronger verbs to take the place of these "weak" verbs.

8. Find an example of the use of each of the five senses and mark it in the text. If you cannot find one of these, mark a place in the essay where it could be inserted.

9. Find a simile or metaphor. If you do not find one, indicate that the writer should insert one.

10. Read each others' essays backwards, sentence by sentence from the end to the beginning, proofreading for punctuation and grammatical errors.

11. Write two or three sentences at the end of the draft that sum up your reaction to the essay.

Conferencing

Another form of workshopping that is very effective is conferencing. Instead of interacting with your peers, conferencing involves meeting with your instructor or a campus Writing Center staff person for a set period of time—usually fifteen or twenty minutes. During your conference, a trained instructor will look over your draft and give you a professional opinion on your revising and editing decisions. These conferences can often help you overcome specific problems you are having with your draft, or help you identify problems and fix them. Take advantage of your campus Writing Center and/or your instructor's office hours; you have a lot to gain and nothing to lose.

2

The Explanatory Essay

Explanatory Essay Overview

The explanatory essay simply explains something. There are many directions an explanatory essay can take, but most are based on the journalistic questions: who, what, why, where, when, and how. Here are some examples of possible topics:

1. An explanation of a process:
   - How to waterski
   - How to choose a pair of running shoes
   - How a computer modem communicates with other computers
2. An explanation of something unfamiliar to the audience:
   - How a virus infects cells in the body
   - What is involved in a college-level debate tournament
   - Who really "discovered" America
3. An analysis of cause and effect:
   - What are the effects of alcohol on the body
   - What causes cerebral palsy
   - What effect college grades have on first-job placement rates

It is important to remember that your paper shouldn't argue a point. You should write a relatively neutral, objective paper that presents interesting information in an understandable way.

Studying the Explanatory Essay

Read the following example of an explanatory essay, and answer the questions. While you read, think about what makes this type of essay different from the narrative. What keeps you interested in the topic? What questions occur to you as you read? Record your reactions by writing notes to yourself in the margins or by keeping a reading journal in which you record your reactions.

Treadmilling
Julie Freeman

Have you been sitting on the couch all winter, keeping Frito Lay in business? Now has come the time to start thinking about the shorts that are packed away in the depths of your closet. How about that swimsuit you vowed yourself you would wear this summer?

Perhaps you have come to the conclusion that it is time for your body to get moving. But what about all those excuses you keep making? A treadmill could be the right exercise equipment for you. The excuses such as bad weather, unsafe neighborhood, waiting for a phone call, or a dislike of sweating in public are all eliminated by using a treadmill in your home (Spilner 2).

The cost of a treadmill has become quite economical. Icon Health and Fitness manufactures most of the treadmills in the United States that sell for less than $1,000. *Consumer Reports* suggests owning a motorized treadmill. Last year the price for a motorized treadmill that is sturdy enough for jogging was priced at more than $2,000. Today the top-of-the-line treadmill sells for only $1,600 (Treadmills 1).

When it comes to purchasing a treadmill, there are many to choose from. A few of the name brands of these machines are Image, Healthrider, Tunturi, Life Fitness, Weslo Cadence, Proform, and Key Fitness. Each of these brands has different models from which to choose, depending on the features you desire (Treadmills 6).

A recent issue of *Consumer Reports* did a comparison of ten different styles of treadmills. Four of these received an excellent rating, five received at least a very good rating, and only one didn't receive a recommendation at all (Treadmills 6).

The Image 10.6Q treadmill was one of the machines that received an overall rating of excellent. This treadmill is equipped with six preset programs and two custom and heart programs. This treadmill received excellent scores in the fit, safety, wear, and monitor categories. It conveniently folds and is quiet during use. The Image 10.6Q has a retail price of $1,600, which is lower than models that received a lower rating (Treadmills 7).

The Tunturi J660 did receive an excellent score, as did the Image 10.6Q. However, this treadmill has a retail price of $2,000, which is $400 more than the Image 10.6Q. This treadmill received an excellent score for wear. It received very good scores in the fit, safety, and monitor categories. The Tunturi J660 has five preset programs and one custom program. This more expensive model does not have a place for a water bottle. The report also indicated that the belt on this treadmill does have the tendency to stop abruptly (Treadmills 8).

The Proform 785 received a very good rating from *Consumer Reports*. This treadmill is retailed at $1,000. It is equipped with six preset programs and two custom and heart programs. The Proform 785 received an excellent score for fit and monitor. However, it did receive only a good score for safety. This report warns that this particular model has a weak latch when folded, so it could cause injury when being moved. A newer model with a better latch should be available soon (Treadmills 8).

The Weslo Cadence 935 received only a good rating. It does not have any programmed features. This treadmill has an incline feature that is adjusted manually. The display monitor is dimly lit, and the speed control is awkward. The only excellent rating was in the wear category. The retail price of this model is only $360 (Treadmills 9).

The Key Fitness Pro900 was not even scored and was not recommended. *Consumer Reports* suggested avoiding this machine because of "the quality control and safety problems" (Treadmills 9).

A person should purchase a treadmill that includes features he or she will use. Some treadmills are equipped with programmed workouts that vary the speed and incline of the machine to simulate hills and maximize the workout. Some machines allow a person to customize and program his or her own workout to use again. Another available feature measures your heart rate with pulse sensors, using your thumb or hand. The incline of the treadmill can be adjusted manually or electronically, depending on the machine. A manual incline is more cumbersome because a person has to get off the machine to make the adjustment. The speed of the treadmill is controlled by pushbuttons or slide switches. If you move a slide switch too fast, you could be thrown off balance. The last feature, which varies with treadmills, is the monitor display. Some monitors display information such as the number of calories burned and the distance and time of each workout. This information is either shown all at once on the panel or on scanning displays that move the information across a window. Most models of treadmills have room for a water bottle and a place for books and magazines; all have side handrails (Treadmills 3).

Weight loss is the number one health benefit gained by using a treadmill. Losing weight helps cut back the risk of cardiovascular disease, diabetes, cancer, and arthritis (Trevor 1). Increasing walking speed can increase weight loss. Research by the Washington University School of Medicine in St. Louis proves that "walkers can burn just as many calories as runners doing the same speed, when they go above 4.5 mph." It also concluded "walkers can burn even more calories than runners at speeds of 5.5 to 6.5 mph—a rugged walking pace" (Spilner 4). Music is the key to get your legs moving. It is suggested that you listen to music that is set to the tempo of the pace you are walking. Any type of music, from a warm up with classical to techno pop, can get a person moving (Spilner 2).

If it has been a while since your body has been motivated to exercise, start your workout slowly. In the first week, walk only for three days for 10 minutes at a speed that is comfortable to you. Each week if you add 5 minutes and one day, by the fourth week you should be walking at least 30 minutes for five days. Also, increase your speed, walking as if you were in a hurry (Trevor 3).

Be aware of potential injuries when using a treadmill. Len Kravitz, Ph.D., a wellness coordinator at the University of Mississppi in Oxford, offers some tips to using a treadmill safely. "To start, carefully step on the belt when it starts to pick up speed. Don't play with a Walkman or your clothes while on the treadmill, and keep your head up to avoid tripping. A good pair of walking shoes should prevent pulled muscles and sore joints. If you are losing your balance, hold on to the handrails. Also make sure to slow the machine down to a complete stop before getting off" (Treading Safely 1). A good way to prevent injuries is to have good walking posture. Drop your shoulders, hold your arms bent at the elbow at an 85- to 90-degree angle and swing them like pendulums, keeping your stomach firm, but remember to breathe. While walking, push off with your back foot and roll from heel to toe. Your feet should be parallel, with the toes and knees pointing forward (Trevor 4).

A treadmill can be easy to afford and convenient to use. With spring just around the corner, get off the couch and throw away those chips. Clear a spot in your basement or bedroom. No more excuses! Grab your Walkman, hop on a treadmill, and get your body moving.

Works Cited

Spilner, Maggie. "Walking Fit." *Prevention*, Dec. 1998: 68+. EBSCO host.

"Treading Safely." *Good Housekeeping*, Mar. 1997: 50. EBSCO host.

"Treadmills." *Consumer Reports*, Feb. 1999: 35+. EBSCO host.

Trevor, Alice. "Walk Off 10, 25, Even 100 pounds!" *Prevention*, Oct. 1998: 112+. EBSCO host.

Questions

1. What is Julie's purpose in writing this essay? What exactly is she attempting to explain? Has she fulfilled her purpose?
2. Find places in the essay where Julie explains concepts or terms, and underline these places.
3. Bracket areas of description in the essay. Why do you think Julie chose to include description in these places, based on the purpose you identified in question 1?

The Explanatory Essay in Everyday Life

Explanatory Activity

To help you understand how you use explanatory strategies in everyday life, complete the following activity. You have twenty minutes to complete the assignment.

1. Define the word "ugly" in your own words, using as much description as necessary.

2. Write down an example of something "ugly" that fits your definition.

3. Pretend that you are explaining "ugly" to someone unfamiliar with the word. The person knows what "pretty" is. Use an example of something "pretty" to illustrate what "ugly" is (hint: you'll be comparing and contrasting two examples).

4. Write a short paragraph based on the answers you gave to the first three questions (Remember to spell-check!)

5. Write a short paragraph explaining how to turn on and log onto a computer at your campus.

6. What caused you to enroll in classes here? What will be the effect of your education on your future life? Write a short paragraph that answers these questions.

Discuss your answers in a small group, focusing on the following questions:

1. Read your "ugly" paragraphs aloud. Comment on your group members' use of description and definition. What image really evokes "ugly"? Why is "ugly" easy to define in such different ways?

2. Read your computer paragraphs aloud. Notice if important details were left out (hint: did anyone forget to turn the computer on?).

3. Finally, compare your answers to the final questions; do you see the cause and effect taking place in each person's life? How does the writer indicate these causes and effects? Why is it possible for so many people to have different answers to this question?

Beginning the Explanatory Essay

Finding a Thesis Statement

A thesis statement is a purpose statement for your essay. In your first essay, the narrative, you may not have included your purpose statement in your essay at all; often, when we write narratives, our purpose is simply to tell a story. In most other types of writing, however, it is customary and necessary to state your topic and purpose in a complete sentence that could stand alone outside of the essay and still make sense. Using the journalist's questions, brainstorm a list of possible topics by quickly filling in the blanks in the following exercise. If you can't think of an answer for one, move on to the next. Try to choose topics you know a little bit about already, and think about your audience; what do *they* want to know about?

What is _____?

How to _____.

_____ causes _____.

_____ is the effect of _____.

This is how a/an _____ is put together.

This is how a/an _____ works.

This is how to install a/an _____.

This is how to take apart a/an _____.

The key to understanding _____ is _____.

Why does _____?

_____ is like _____.

_____ is not like _____.

I know how to _____.

I know why _____.

I know what a/an _____ is.

From the exercise above, or on your own, come up with a thesis statement for your explanatory paper. Remember to change questions into statements; a thesis statement should answer, not ask, a question.

Narrowing Your Thesis

To make sure your thesis is narrow enough, answer the following questions and reformulate your thesis, incorporating as much as possible of the information you generated through the questions.

1. Who, specifically, is involved in the topic of this paper?

2. Where, specifically, is this topic set?

3. What, exactly, are you going to explain?

4. Why is this topic interesting or important?

5. In what time frame and setting is this topic taking place?

After you have answered the previous five questions in detail, get into groups and talk about your answers. After you have discussed some possibilities with your classmates and/or instructor, reformulate your thesis so that it is specific and to the point.

Strategies of Development

Description   This was the primary method of development you were supposed to use in your narrative essay. Good description involves all five senses (sight, hearing, smell, taste, and touch), and may involve the use of simile and/or metaphor.

Definition   Let's begin with what definition is *not*. Definition is *not* taking a dictionary or encyclopedia definition and writing a paper based on this definition. Instead, the writer *re*-defines what it is he or she is writing about. The writer may narrow the definition, expand it, or re-think it entirely. For example, a writer could define an abstract word like "progress" in the following ways:

Progress is: a. industry and technology that provides us with a bet-
                 ter life.
               b. industrialization that pollutes our land, air, and water.
               c. moving forward with well-thought-out personal goals.

Process Analysis   Process analysis involves step-by-step subdivision of a process. This process can be as complicated as how AIDS invades the body; it can be as simple as how to change a diaper. The important thing to remember in process analysis is that the description of the process must proceed in chronological order and must be thorough. A process analysis is still an essay, not a set of directions, so transitions are quite necessary.

Comparison/Contrast   Comparison/contrast shows the relationship that exists between two people, places, things, or ideas. A comparison shows the similarities between the two entities; a contrast shows the differences. Two methods are used in comparison and contrast: block style and alternating style.

Block Style: In block style, one paragraph explains the first entity and the next paragraph compares and contrasts the first entity to the second, while explaining the second.

For example, if a writer were writing a comparison/contrast of peas and carrots, and the first point of comparison/contrast was color and texture, this is what block style would look like:

Peas grow above the ground and are encased in green pods. When the pod is opened, the small green peas can be seen, each one connected to the pod by a stringy green substance. Raw peas are hard, and can be rolled between the first finger and thumb like marbles.

Carrots, on the other hand, grow beneath the ground and are orange. When pulled from the ground, stringy orange roots may stick out from the main root, the carrot. Carrots are long and thin, and range in size from finger size (baby carrots) to twelve inches in length.

Alternating Style: In alternating style, comparison/contrast is done within the same paragraph. See the example below, which uses the same topic as the block example above:

> Peas grow above the ground and are encased in green pods. Carrots, on the other hand, grow beneath the ground and are orange. When pulled from the ground, stringy orange roots may stick out from the main root, the carrot. Peas, however, grow in pods. When the pod is opened, the small green peas can be seen, connected to the pod by a stringy green substance.

Classification and Division   Classification and division involves breaking down a complex idea into simple parts. By classifying and dividing a topic, the writer can make a large subject seem less intimidating. For example, by classifying a car as a sports car and then describing what makes that car a sports car, a writer can explain the features of that car much better.

Cause and Effect   Cause and effect is a method of development used to explain why an event occurred or what the consequences of an action will be.

The key to a good explanation is examples. If you have good examples of the concept you are trying to explain, your reader is more likely to understand the point you are trying to get across.

Strategies of Development: Which Ones Do I Use?

Answer the questions below about your chosen thesis:

1. How will you define key terms and points in your essay?

2. If you use jargon and phrases that aren't generally familiar, how will you explain them?

3. What are important characteristics of your topic or explanation? (Use descriptive techniques from the narrative paper.)

4. Think about the process you've chosen; in what order will you introduce concepts?

5. How can you create meaning by using something familiar to explain the unfamiliar (compare/contrast)?

6. How would you classify and divide your topic in the larger or smaller system to which it belongs?

7. What are the effects of your topic on your audience? What are the causes of your topic?

Look over your answers to these questions, and decide which strategies of development would work best in your paper. You will probably use two or three to explain your topic.

Using Sources in the Explanatory Essay

Many times, in order to explain something fully, we must use outside sources: books, magazine articles, Web pages, and interviews are all common sources students use to support the thesis statement and topic sentences of their essays.

Not just any old source will do. Maybe in high school your teachers allowed you to use encyclopedias or dictionaries as primary sources in your essays; that sort of thing is frowned upon in college. Finding qualified, dependable sources isn't easy. Often it takes time to find the kinds of sources you will need to support your points. That's why it is very important that you learn how to use your library's computerized cataloging system to find books, magazine articles, and Web pages.

Researching sources takes place throughout the writing process. You may want to begin researching before you begin outlining or drafting, to find out what information is available to you. We call this sort of research preliminary research because it takes place before much is written. After you have written your outline, you will probably find yourself researching again to fill in the gaps or add to the points you are making. This is perfectly normal; in fact, it's almost impossible to avoid.

Boolean Search Terms, or Boolean Operators

Some library systems and almost all Web search engines, such as Webcrawler (**www.webcrawler.com**) and Excite (**www.excite.com**), allow users to search with boolean operators. These words make it easier for students to find specific information in the library and on the Web. Here are the main boolean operators and their meanings:

AND +   Using "AND" or "+" between two words indicates that both words must appear in the source you are looking for. For example, if you wanted to find an article about monkeys in Brazil, you could type this boolean phrase: monkeys AND Brazil.

OR /   Using "OR" or "/" between two words indicates that either word can appear in the source you are looking for. For example, if you wanted to find an article about chimpanzees or gorillas, you could type this boolean phrase: chimpanzees OR gorillas.

NEAR   Using NEAR between two words indicates that the two words should appear near each other in the source. For example, "literature NEAR Mexico" would probably find sources that dealt with Mexican literature.

NOT   Using "NOT" or "–" between two words will eliminate the second word. (Some search engines require AND NOT instead). For example if you were searching for information on elephants other than Asian elephants, this phrase might work: "elephants" AND NOT "Asian."

( ) and " "   Depending on the search engine, you can use parentheses and/or quotation marks to identify phrases that must appear in the sources. For example, if you typed in the phrase "Marilyn Monroe" or (Marilyn Monroe), you would find sources with the words Marilyn and Monroe right next to one another. However, if you typed in "Marilyn AND Monroe" you would also find sources that just happened to have both words in them somewhere—in other words, sources that might have nothing to do with your topic.

Practice using boolean operators on the Web and in your library. To find sources that support your topic sentences and thesis statement, analyze your outline. Choose words and phrases that appear in your outline, and type these words and phrases using boolean terms. You'll find sources a lot faster!

Boolean Operator Practice

Write boolean search phrases for the following search problems. After you have written some potential search phrases, try them out on the Web and see which combinations work the best.

1. You've decided to write a paper about science fiction, focusing on the work of Jules Verne.

2. You're researching the effects lead has on the human body.

3. You want to find a site on the musical *The King and I* that also includes information about one of its stars, Deborah Kerr.

4. You're looking for sources that address A. A. Milne's *Winnie the Pooh,* but you want to eliminate any sites that include information on Disney's version of Pooh.

5. You're looking for a recipe for strawberry jam that doesn't require cooking.

6. You're searching for articles about the book *Tom Jones,* not the entertainer/singer Tom Jones.

7. You need to find some information on a career as a computer programmer, including salary, college requirements, and job prospects.

8. You want to find sources about the causes of HIV/AIDS that were written in 1996.

9. You need sources on euthanasia or mercy killing, but you don't want any sources mentioning Dr. Kevorkian.

10. You're looking for a site that provides weather information for Canada.

Evaluating Sources

As we said before, not every source is good enough to use in a college-level paper. Here are some questions to ask yourself about each source you consider for use in your paper:

1. Who is the author of the source? What education or experience does the author have with the topic?

2. Where was the source published? By whom? Does this person or organization have any known biases that could affect the truth or validity of the information you want to use?

3. When was the source published? Is it outdated? Is it too new to have any solid facts?

First, if your source doesn't name an author, you need to make sure that it was written by a reputable and informed person. This is especially true of Web pages, since anyone is free to express opinions on the Web, whether qualified to do so or not. It is also important to note where the document was published and by whom. Certain clubs and organizations may have agendas that lead them to irrelevant or biased conclusions. Lastly, make sure your source is new enough to contain valuable information. A source that is more than ten years old is probably too old to be of much value. If in doubt, ask your instructor.

Review Activity

Turn to Julie Freeman's essay in the section of this chapter titled Studying the Explanatory Essay. Then complete the exercises below.

1. Underline the thesis statement in the introduction and conclusion.

2. Study the essay carefully, and identify where the writer uses different strategies of development. For example, if you notice a paragraph that uses comparison/contrast alternating style, bracket the paragraph and write "comparison/contrast alternating" in the margin.

3. After you have completed the first two questions, analyze the essay. Where would you have used a different strategy of development? Why?

4. What research materials were incorporated into the essay? How were the sources used to support the topic sentences and thesis statement?

5. Get into a group with your classmates and compare your answers. Discuss the changes you would make in the essay and why.

Drafting the Explanatory Essay

Outlining

Planning is an important aspect of the explanatory essay. It's usually not a good idea to start drafting this essay without an outline. Most of the time, if you can't complete an outline, you aren't ready to write the rough draft. Get some help from your campus writing lab or your instructor if you're having trouble with your outline.

A good outline consists of a thesis statement and complete topic sentences. A topic sentence is the main idea of a paragraph to be developed. Look at your notes from the previous section's exercises. Write an outline for your explanatory essay based on your notes, filling in the following blanks.

 I. Introduction: Thesis statement: _____

 II. Topic Sentence: _____

 III. Topic Sentence: _____

 IV. Topic Sentence: _____

 V. Topic Sentence: _____

 VI. Topic Sentence: _____

 VII. Conclusion: Thesis Statement: _____

Note: The number of topic sentences can vary from essay to essay, depending on the length of the assignment. Consult with your instructor about the number of recommended topic sentences in the body of the essay.

Incorporating Sources into the Explanatory Essay

There are three ways to cite sources in your essay: direct quotation, paraphrase, and summary.

Direct Quotation Use direct quotation only when the original wording is superb or when the original words are absolutely necessary to convey the intended meaning. A direct quote is surrounded by quotation marks.

Here are four common ways to present and punctuate quotes:

1. Work the quote into the sentence in a grammatically correct manner.

> Martin Luther King indicates that "in any nonviolent campaign there are four basic steps: collection of the facts to determine whether injustices exist; negotiation; self-purification; and direct action."

2. Preface the quote with a phrase.

> Martin Luther King states, "In any nonviolent campaign there are four basic steps: collection of the facts to determine whether injustices exist; negotiation; self-purification; and direct action."

3. Preface the quote with a statement.

Martin Luther King indicates his beliefs on the process of an effective protest: "In any nonviolent campaign there are four basic steps: collection of the facts to determine whether injustices exist; negotiation; self-purification; and direct action."

4. Follow the quote with a phrase.

"In any nonviolent campaign there are four basic steps: collection of the facts to determine whether injustices exist; negotiation; self-purification; and direct action," states Martin Luther King.

Paraphrase   Paraphrase most of the information you will use in your essay. A paraphrase is simply a translation of the ideas in the original source into your own words. It is roughly the same length as the original material.

> Martin Luther King's four steps to a nonviolent campaign include searching for and verifying injustices, negotiating, purifying of the self, and, finally, taking action.

Summary   When you run into a large amount of material (a page or more) that you want to include in your essay in abbreviated form, summarize. A summary is a much shorter, condensed version of the original source material.

> Martin Luther King's "Letter from Birmingham Jail" addresses King's fellow clergymen and explains both his previous actions and his vision of a truly free America.

The first time you use a source in an essay, whether you quote, paraphrase, or summarize, you should use a running acknowledgment that indicates the author's name and credentials. In the case of an extremely well-known activist such as Martin Luther King, this isn't necessary. However, most of your sources will be written by more obscure writers. There are three ways to write running acknowledgments:

1. At the beginning of a sentence:

Dr. Sandra Long, pediatrician, indicates that many children who attend public schools are not immunized properly against childhood diseases.

2. In the middle of a sentence:

Many children in public schools, according to Dr. Sandra Long, pediatrician, are not properly immunized against childhood diseases.

3. At the end of a sentence:

Many children in public schools are not properly immunized against childhood diseases, states Dr. Sandra Long, pediatrician.

MLA Documentation Style

MLA Documentation Style is a method that students use to give credit to sources. Whether you quote, paraphrase, or summarize, you must use MLA style to give credit to the source from which you took the material.

MLA style is much easier to use than its predecessor, footnotes. In the main text, or body, of your essay, you will use parenthetical citations. Here are two examples:

Direct quote:

Toby Fulwiler offers this tip to writers who struggle with topics that are too large: "Another way to fight overgeneralization is to limit time and place" (322).

Paraphrase:

Restricting temporal and spatial parameters is a technique writers may use to narrow a topic (Fulwiler 322).

The two examples above also illustrate another aspect of MLA style. When the author's name appears in the sentence, it is not necessary to insert it in the parentheses at the end of the sentence; if the author's name does not appear in the sentence, you must insert it in the parentheses after the sentence.

You must also write a Works Cited page, which will be the last page of your essay and will list all the other necessary information about your sources. The Works Cited page is alphabetized according to the authors' last names, so that a reader can read an author's name in the parentheses and then flip forward to the final page and find the source information. Here's a sample Works Cited entry for the book referred to previously.

Fulwiler, Toby. *The Working Writer*. Englewood Cliffs, NJ: Prentice Hall, 1995.

Works Cited entries for books, magazines, and Web pages are all written differently. For a complete index of Works Cited entry examples and in-text examples, refer to the Web pages listed in the Web page appendix under Explanatory Essay Links, or refer to a good handbook.

Using Sources

The most important thing to remember when using sources in an essay is that the sources should *support*, not *make*, your points. Some students become so enraptured with their sources that they quote, paraphrase, and summarize too much. They use sources to make their case, rather than arguing it themselves. When using sources in an essay, remember that you are using the sources to support your case. As a lawyer calls witnesses to the stand, you will use sources to help make your case, or support your points.

After you've chosen some good quotes, paraphrases, and summaries to incorporate into your explanatory essay, revise your outline. Insert the quotes, paraphrases, and summaries into the points where they will appear; make sure you also write your in-text citations in the MLA style too, so that you don't have to look it up again later. Think about transition words you will use, such as "for example" and "according to."

Drafting

Once you have written an outline, the drafting of this essay is easy. Use your outline as the "skeleton" of your essay. Add details, using the strategies of development discussed earlier, to make your essay interesting and specific. Don't worry too much about the introduction and conclusion at first; ideally, you'll write those last, anyway. Just get the body of your essay down for your rough draft.

Writing the Introduction

Sometimes students work so hard on their essays that they forget the most important part: the introduction. Without an interest-grabbing introduction, your paper will fall flat. Who would want to read an essay that begins like this?

> AIDS is a deadly disease that threatens people's lives. Many people don't think about getting AIDS; they think that only other people get AIDS. The way the AIDS virus invades the body is amazing.

Pretty blah, huh? What about this one?

> Sandy squinched her eyes shut as she stabbed the needle into her arm. Slowly, in painful ecstasy, she eased the heroin into her bloodstream. When the plunger was all the way down, Sandy hesitated, then carefully drew it out of her arm. She smiled, set the needle on the table, and leaned back onto the couch.

> "Hey Sandy, can I bum a needle off ya?" Mark sat down next to her.
>
> "That was my last one." Sandy pointed to the needle on the table.
>
> "That's OK by me." Mark picked up the needle and pulled a vial out of his pocket; he filled it up, injected himself, and settled onto the couch with Sandy.
>
> This is how AIDS invades the human body.

Or this one?

> According to the UNAIDS: Report on the Global HIV/AIDS Epidemic, 30.6 million people worldwide—29.5 million adults and 1.1 million children younger than 15 years—were living with HIV/AIDS at the close of 1997 (NIAD). The death toll is staggering, especially when one considers the way the HIV and AIDS infect the human body.*

As you can see, it's pretty easy to jazz up a boring introduction and make it shine. All you need is a vivid story or a hard-hitting statistic, right? Well, not exactly. Introductory techniques should be based on the topic being explained in the essay; for instance, if your essay is about constructing a park bench, chances are you won't be able to find a startling statistic to use in your introduction. There are many ways to generate interest in a topic. Take a look at the list below, and think about your essay topic. Which technique looks like a good fit? Try out a couple and see which one works best.

- Asking questions
- Giving the history of the topic
- Using a recent news story that relates to the topic
- Relating a story from your own past that relates to the topic
- Describing a scene
- Defining the key terms in the essay

Fitting It All Together: Transitions

Dylan and Rebecca decided to buy a new sofa. They saved money so that they could have a sofa made to their specifications. Dylan and Rebecca spent time with the craftsman, explaining how they wanted the sofa to

---

*Cited from: National Institute of Allergy and Infections Disease (NIAD) Fact Sheet http://www.niaid.nih.gov/factsheets/aidsstat.htm (October 1998).

look, drawing pictures of the final product, and choosing fabric for the upholstery. The day finally arrived when the sofa was finished. Excitedly, Dylan and Rebecca rushed to the sofa maker's workshop, only to find their sofa in pieces! The legs were neatly stacked in a corner; the upholstered seat cushions were in a pile nearby; the arms and back of the sofa rested against the wall.

"What's the meaning of this?" Dylan demanded. Rebecca stood nearby, speechless.

The sofa maker looked puzzled. "I made everything according to your specifications."

"All the pieces look beautiful," Rebecca said calmly. "But they're just pieces. The sofa's not put together right." Rebecca pointed to the seat cushions, then to the legs, arms, and back. "How are we supposed to use it?"

Believe it or not, this story is a metaphor for poor writing. Many students work hard to polish and revise their paragraphs and to write interesting introductions and conclusions, just as the sofa maker worked hard to make functional legs, cushions, arms, and a back for the sofa. After finishing these tasks, students may feel their essays are finished. However, like the sofa maker, they have forgotten the most important thing: putting the pieces together.

Three Transitional Methods   There are three commonly used methods of connecting paragraphs of an essay together. These methods are (1) weaving ideas; (2) using transitional words; and (3) using pronouns.

The most effective transitional method involves weaving ideas from the previous paragraph into ideas to be presented in the current paragraph. To practice writing transitions in this manner, print out your current draft and cut out each paragraph. Set the paragraphs on the floor in order, so you can read the essay from beginning to end.

Look at the final few sentences of your introduction, and the first few sentences of your first body paragraph. Try writing a couple of sentences which incorporate ideas from both paragraphs. When you find one that you like, tape it between the two paragraphs. Now, go on to the end of the first body paragraph and the beginning of the second body paragraph and repeat the process until you have finished the essay. Go back to the computer and add in your transitions at the beginning of each paragraph. This activity also works well if you complete it with a couple of classmates, because you may be able to give each other some good ideas for transition sentences.

Another method of writing transitions involves using transitional "signal" words to indicate the relationship between the ideas in the forthcoming paragraph and the ideas in the previous paragraph. Some common transition words include:

> *Transitions involving time:* after, then, before, during
>
> *Transitions involving space:* around, above, below, under, over
>
> *Transitions involving exceptions:* however, on the other hand, despite, still
>
> *Transitions involving additions:* also, likewise, moreover, furthermore, too

Many handbooks and online handbooks contain large lists of these words; this is only a small sample of transition words. Be careful not to overuse or misuse this method. It is very important that you use transitional words that make sense and truly represent the relationship between paragraphs or sentences. You can practice using this method using the same "cut and tape" method suggested above.

The final method of signaling a transition is to use pronouns that refer to people, places, things, or ideas that were mentioned in the previous paragraph. This method must be used quite early in a paragraph to be effective. It is easy to overuse this method, so use it sparingly.

Remember, the most effective method of writing transitions involves taking the time to weave ideas from paragraph to paragraph. While it takes less time to choose an appropriate transition word or to use pronouns to refer to ideas presented earlier, these final two methods aren't as effective or as interesting.

Revising the Explanatory Essay

Here is a peer review editing guide for the explanatory essay. Use this guide to improve, revise, and edit your classmates' drafts and your own. Also, don't forget to conference with your instructor or a staff member at your campus writing center.

Explanatory Essay Peer Edit

1. Trade drafts with someone else in class. Then go step by step through the following procedure, marking on the person's paper when appropriate.

2. Read the essay carefully for content. If there are parts you don't understand, mark them. When both of you are done marking, discuss any areas that are confusing and suggest changes that would make the essay clearer and more understandable.

3. Underline the thesis statement in both the introduction and conclusion. If you can't find the thesis statement, indicate that one needs to be inserted.

4. Underline the topic sentences of all the paragraphs (a topic sentence is the purpose statement of the paragraph and is usually either the first or last sentence of a paragraph).

5. Now, look at the sentences you underlined to help you determine what strategies of development the writer has used.

6. Put stars next to areas where the writer has defined key terms or concepts. If a term or concept is mentioned but not defined, write "need definition" in the margin.

7. Mark areas where the writer has used comparison/contrast (to explain the unfamiliar by comparing and contrasting it to the familiar) by writing "compare/contrast" in the margin. Notice if the comparison/contrast is effective or not. Does the comparison help you understand, or does it confuse you? If it's confusing, mark it as such.

8. Look for sensory description, and mark good descriptions with "good description." If some parts need more description to clarify meaning, mark "need more description."

9. Notice whether the writer is classifying or dividing his or her topic to make it more understandable. If so, put a dotted line under the classifying or dividing language.

10. Does the author offer explanations of causes and effects relating to his or her topic? If so, circle the areas where the writer does so. Check the writer's evidence closely. Does the writer present enough believable evidence? If not, write "need more evidence."

11. Look for transitions between ideas and paragraphs. If the essay is choppy and needs transitions either within a paragraph or between paragraphs, mark "need transitions."

12. Proof the essay, reading sentence by sentence from the end to the beginning, checking for run-on sentences, fragments, punctuation errors, misused words, and so on.

3

The Evaluative/Interpretive Essay

Evaluative/Interpretive Essay Overview

An evaluative and/or interpretive essay requires that you, the writer, examine and analyze something and make a value judgment. For instance, a movie review is a common evaluative form that we read in magazines or newspapers; the critic watches the movie and then evaluates it, letting the reader know whether, in the critic's opinion, the movie is worth seeing.

Evaluation is not a simple process. An evaluative review of a movie can't just assert that "the movie was good" or "the movie was bad" and not give any reasons for the opinion. Every value judgment must be justified with a definition of what "good" means to the writer and with illustrations/examples from the movie. In other words, an evaluative writer must have criteria that he or she uses to come to his or her conclusions about whatever it is he or she is evaluating.

Evaluating in Everyday Life

Evaluating involves making decisions about the value of something—an object, an experience, a book, an article, an action, an inaction, and so on. You use evaluative thinking every day. For example, when you get up in the morning and decide which outfit to wear, you evaluate your options (Should I wear the red sweater or blue sweater?) and make a choice (The red sweater is warmer, so I'll wear the red sweater).

We don't all make the same evaluations of the same things. For example, if given the choice of any car in the world to drive, some people would choose a Volkswagen bug and some people would choose a 1933 Ford coupe. Why are there differences in the way people evaluate? Because everyone operates from a different value system, which means that they are implementing different *criteria*.

Criteria are the priorities we set in relation to the thing we are evaluating. For example, if you were buying a car, your criteria might be: price, color, engine size, year of manufacture, and stereo system. If your grandma were buying a car, her criteria might be: large size, quiet engine, low maintenance costs, and heated steering wheel. Who you are and what your priorities are define your criteria.

Not many people are conscious of the criteria they are using all the time. For instance, we all have criteria when it comes to choosing a significant other, but unless we have tried to write down those criteria, we might not know exactly what they are. We might say things like "I'm looking for someone nice." But that statement really doesn't tell anybody anything. Marilyn Manson's definition of "nice" and your definition of "nice" may not be the same. So it's important to specifically define your criteria, not just use words like "good" or "bad."

Library Activity—Evaluative Essay   Find a restaurant or movie review. You will probably find reviews in your local newspaper or in a national magazine. The quickest way to find reviews is to use your library's magazine search catalog. Ask the librarian for assistance if you don't know how to use your library's magazine database or catalog.

Answer the questions below, based on the review you find.

Article Title: _____   Author: _____

Magazine: _____   Date: _____

1. How does the author feel about the topic? Write the thesis statement below.

2. What strategies of development does the author use? (Refer to your notes if necessary.)

3. What background information on the topic is presented in the introduction?

4. Is the conclusion strong or weak? Does the author's opinion appear there?

5. Would you characterize the author's writing style as formal or informal? Does he or she use jargon or technical terms?

6. What criteria has the author used to come to his or her opinion? Is the criteria objective or subjective? Do you think the criteria is significant or not?

   7. Write an example of when the author backed up his or her argument with an example.

   8. What is the author's strongest point? Weakest point?

   9. Is the article one-sided, or does the author present both good and bad characteristics?

Studying the Evaluative Paper (Restaurant Review)

Panda Garden Buffet
Gina Ryan

No longer a carefree teenager with money burning holes in my pockets, I require something a little out of the ordinary to entice me to part with my money at mealtime. While I deplore the time and effort required to make myself and my family a filling, nutritious meal, I have an equally hard time justifying the expenditure of eighty cents for one egg at a local restaurant when I can buy the whole dozen for the same price at the supermarket.

   This is why I tend to go for either the more exotic types of foods or an upscale atmosphere when I do eat out; if I'm going to pay the price, I want something that I cannot provide for myself at home. Thus, I invited my family to join me for Chinese at the newest Chinese restaurant in town, Panda Garden Buffet.

   Panda Garden Buffet is located at 708 North Ankeny Boulevard, just a block north of Hy-Vee. When I noticed the somewhat gaudy sign at the entrance (yellow background with black and red lettering and pictures of panda with bamboo), I expected to walk into a typical fast-food Chinese restaurant. Upon entering, I was surprised not to immediately spy the expected counter, cash register, and cheap square tables with red vinyl cushioned chairs and the standard buffet typical of a fast-food Chinese joint. Instead, there was carpeting (!) and a wall running almost the entire width of the store. On the wall (also carpeted) was a huge back-lighted photograph of what appeared to be a Buddhist temple. Following the wall to the left, we found a hallway that led to the expected cash register and what appeared to be an order counter. As we got closer to the smiling Asian man at the counter, we realized that the dining room was considerably larger than we had expected. The man at the counter inquired as to the number in our party and sat us at a booth close to one of the two buffets.

A congenial waitress appeared as soon as we were settled. She took our drink orders and offered us the choice of ordering from the menu or partaking of the buffet. We chose to take a look at both before deciding.

The menu was definitely appealing. With over one hundred meals to choose from, as well as seventeen appetizers and soups, there is certainly something for everyone. There are thirty-three Chef's Specials alone, a few of which are actually described. My pet peeve with many exotic restaurants is the lack of detailed description of menu items; unfortunately, Panda Garden Buffet is one of many such establishments that apparently expect one to psychically *know* what is in each dish.

Many entrees are available in either a small or large portion. The prices appeared quite reasonable, ranging from as low as $2.95 for a small portion of Vegetable Fried Rice to $10.95 for the Seafood Delight, a Mandarin-style Chef's Special that includes "fresh jumbo shrimp, scallops, king crab meat, and Chinese vegetables." Lunch specials (available from 10:30 a.m. to 3:00 p.m.) run $4.15 a plate, and combination platters are $6.15. A buffet costs $4.99 at lunchtime and $6.99 at dinner.

Three of us elected to sample the buffet, while one die-hard Mu Shu Pork fan held out for her favorite. Panda Garden Buffet features two buffets, one for cold foods and one for hot. The cold food buffet holds several types of fresh and canned fruits, pasta salads, and lettuce, but no toppings other than a couple of dressings. I was impressed to find chunks of mango mixed in with what appeared to be canned mixed fruit. Creamed green peas were also available on this bar.

The hot buffet bar had soups (egg drop and hot and sour), appetizers such as the obligatory egg rolls and crab rangoon, and the main dishes. Garlic Chicken, Mixed Lo Mein, Double-Cooked Pork, and Sautéed Mixed Vegetables were among some of the entrees available. Also vying for plate space were meatballs mixed in a sweet and sour sauce, crab legs, and sweet and sour pork.

The Mu Shu Pork fanatic was jealously drooling over our bountifully filled plates for only a short while before she received a *heaping* plate of Mu Shu and five folded white pancakes with plum sauce. Then it was our turn to drool. The buffet food was for the most part pretty good—with the exception of the hot and sour soup, which was rather flavorless. The Mu Shu Pork was a perfect mixture of pork, fried egg, and various vegetables; this dish was served fresh and hot. I have heard this dish described best as the "Chinese Burrito"; the plum sauce is spread on the pancakes, which are like paper-thin tortillas.

Our server was friendly and attentive, often anticipating our needs. She refilled drinks before we could think to ask, and kept the dirty dishes on our table to a minimum. She also spent some time talking to the four-year-old in our party, who by the end of the evening had decided he didn't hate Chinese quite as much as he'd previously insisted. Hot food was hot, cold food was cold, and all the foods appeared and smelled appetizing. The only problem I had with the place was the atmosphere. It couldn't seem to decide if it was a very classy fast-food joint, or a cheap attempt at an elegant restaurant. For instance, the lighting consisted mainly of the round, recessed lights found in Burger King, but there were four ceiling fans with tulip-glass encased bulbs, and there appeared to be a chandelier in the back dining room. The booths were a mint green vinyl, the tables marble-patterned Formica, but the chairs sported a rather snazzy black frame with art nouveau vinyl in a pattern of black, pink, and red. The booths were divided with carpeted walls, over which were hung glass dividers with various etched pictures.

The walls were covered with a seagull-patterned cloth, and there were a couple of the giant back-lighted photographs with nature scenes. The lack of music seemed almost obtrusive. The bathroom was huge, but the floors and mirrors struck me as being very dirty, especially considering the short time the restaurant had been open.

The tops of the buffets were forested with a great variety of plastic flowers, perhaps to evoke the "garden" in the restaurant's name. Either the signs for the buffet items have yet to arrive, or the money has run out. Items on the buffet were labeled with ink on notebook paper, which was taped to the sneeze guard above the corresponding items. There is some charm to these style discrepancies, however. I particularly enjoyed the "Fried Toast" sign above the deep-fried refrigerator biscuits dipped in granulated sugar.

When all is said and done, I can honestly say I enjoyed my experience at Panda Garden Buffet and would be willing to go back. What is lacking in ambiance is more than made up for in friendly service, the appetizing food, and the very reasonable prices. Even the confused atmosphere has charm. As the front of the menu notes: "All Parties Order Are Welcome. New Beautify Dinning Room Available."

Questions

1. Based on Gina's impressions, would you dine at China Garden Buffet? Why or why not? Be specific in your answer.
2. Where could Gina have been more specific in her description? What are your questions about the restaurant after reading her review?
3. Where was Gina most descriptive? What does this tell the reader about what is important to Gina in a restaurant?

Writing a Restaurant Review

Most of us have a lifetime's worth of experience evaluating food. You probably remember your most hated food from childhood. Was it broccoli? mushrooms? brussel sprouts? Maybe you enjoy those foods today, maybe not. Your criteria for choosing good food has probably changed greatly from the time you were a small child.

Though we all have specific likes and dislikes when it comes to food, many of us have never analyzed what *exactly* we expect when we dine out. For example, some people like a friendly, casual server who converses with them throughout the meal; others of us prefer to be left alone unless the server's presence is absolutely necessary. Obviously, we all have different tastes and preferences; but in order to write a good evaluative review, we must first isolate exactly what our preferences are. A good way to find out what your criteria are to ask yourself the questions: who, what, why, where, when, and how.

Think about going out to a restaurant to eat lunch, and then answer the following questions:

1. Name your favorite restaurant. Why is it your favorite restaurant?

2. When you go to a restaurant, what kind of ambiance do you like? (Think of sound, looks, smell, touch, cleanness, smoking, etc.)

3. What is your favorite food? What is your least favorite food? What do you like about the way your favorite food is prepared?

4. What kind of service do you like best—table service or buffet? What kinds of server behavior do you prefer?

5. How fast should your service be? What should the server offer you or bring automatically?

6. What about location? Where should the restaurant be?

7. Think of the ideal menu. What kinds of items would be on your ideal menu? How would the menu be designed?

8. What kinds of desserts do you like? What is your favorite dessert? How do you like it to be prepared?

9. Why do you like to eat out? Why don't you like to eat out?

10. How much should your server know about the menu?

11. How should the management deal with the situation when you are dissatisfied?

12. What is your preferred method of payment at a restaurant?

Look at your answers to the above questions. Now, isolate what your expectations are for each part of the dining experience. Make a list of your preferences. Here's an example:

Favorite type of restaurant: expensive, elegant

What I expect of a server: fast, courteous service, knowledgeable about specials and menu items, not overly attentive, water glass kept full.

Write a set of at least twelve criteria based on your answers above (feel free to add criteria as you wish).

Take your notebook and eat at the restaurant, recording your value judgments on your criteria as you eat. For example, if one of your criteria was "soft classical music" and the restaurant played loud country music, you would probably record that your criteria was not met because the restaurant was playing country music. Also be sure to record the exact name of the dish you order, and describe your food using five-sense description.

While you are eating and taking notes, remember that in your review you will be expected to give specific examples of how your criteria were or weren't met. It won't be acceptable just to write "the service was fast." You must prove the service was fast in some way. You could record the time you ordered the food and the time the food came to the table, and indicate the exact amount of time it took for the food to arrive; or you could describe the way the server dashed around the dining area. It is not enough just to state your criteria and that they were met; you must also *prove* the criteria were met with specific examples.

Evaluating a Restaurant

1. Look at your notes and identify your criteria. Make a list of the things you "judged" on your visit to the restaurant (for example: service, cleanliness, food quality, etc.).

2. Now divide your criteria into subcategories (for example: Service— 1. speed of seating and greeting; 2. speed of service; 3. friendliness of server; etc.)

3. From the lists generated in the above two questions, make an outline or map of your essay, putting related criteria next to one another.

4. Now take a look at your informal outline. For each criterion, you will have at least one paragraph (for some criteria with numerous subcategories, you will have more than one paragraph). Choose one criterion and begin drafting, following these guidelines:

a. Define your criterion first. What exactly do you mean by "good" service, for instance? You need to define your ideas and expectations of quality to your audience.

b. After you have defined your criterion, explain how the restaurant did or didn't meet it; use description and other strategies of development to achieve this goal (you can use comparison/contrast by comparing this restaurant to another one; you can use cause-and-effect logic; you can classify this restaurant based on its performance—it's really up to you).

c. Description is very important in an evaluative essay because your audience is depending on you to provide descriptive evidence as to why you did or didn't like something. Check over your paragraphs for description of both the criterion and how the restaurant met or didn't meet it.

5. When you are finished writing all your paragraphs, formulate a thesis statement; did you like the restaurant or not? Why or why not? You may want to list your criteria in the thesis statement. In an evaluative essay, you may leave the thesis statement out of the introduction if you like, and put it at the end as a summary statement of your essay.

6. After you have formulated your thesis statement, write an introduction and conclusion.

Restaurant/Movie Review Peer Edit

Trade essays with a partner and answer the following questions, either on their draft or on this page.

1. Read the essay carefully. Does it make sense? Does it flow logically? Mark parts where you get confused; mark repetitive areas.

2. Check for transition words or devices. If the essay lurches along, with no connection between paragraphs, write "Need transitions" somewhere on the page.

3. Underline each criterion and its definition in each paragraph. If you can't find one or the other, note this in the margin.

4. Look at the examples the writer gives. Can you tell if the writer's expectations were met? If there is not enough description to justify the writer's impressions of the restaurant, indicate this in the margins.

5. Analyze the introduction and the conclusion. Does an evaluative thesis statement appear in the conclusion? If not, indicate that one should be there. Has the writer used an introductory technique and a closing technique? If not, suggest one (from your book or on-line handbook).

6. What strategies of development can you identify in this essay (comparison/contrast; classification/division; cause and effect; description; definition)? Which strategy could the writer employ that he or she hasn't utilized?

7. Proofread the essay for slang words. Circle any.

8. Starting at the end of the essay, read the last sentence, second to last sentence, and so on proofreading for run-on sentences, fragments, and errors in punctuation, grammar, spelling, and syntax.

Evaluative Essay—Movie Review

Imagine that you have recently been hired as a clerk in a video store. The manager has decided to put together a book of movie reviews for her customers, so she has assigned each clerk several movies to review. She gives you the following list of criteria to help you review the movie:

1. Plot: Is the plot interesting? Does it move fast enough? Was it predictable? What is the conflict presented in the movie?

2. Genre: Is the movie aimed at a certain audience? How would you classify the movie?

3. Symbolism: Does the movie contain symbols of good and evil? How are symbols presented?

4. Violence: Is this movie suitable for children? Does it make a statement for or against violence?

5. Comedy: Is this movie funny? Does it rely on physical humor or off-color jokes? Would you classify the humor as mature or immature?

6. Characterization: Are the characters believable? Do the actors do a good job of bringing them to life? If so, how?

Formulate an evaluative essay that is a movie review, based on the information you've gathered above. Make sure you mention and *define* all the criteria the video store manager asked for in your review. Also, you should rate the film according to the following scale:

**** = very good

*** = good

**   = could have been better

*   = not worth seeing

Remember to include a thesis statement in the introduction and conclusion. The conclusion will probably contain the rating information and your final opinion about the film.

When you have finished a draft of your movie review, use the Restaurant/Movie Review Peer Edit assignment to help you with your revisions.

The Interpretive Essay: Interpreting Literature

Interpreting is slightly different from evaluating, though the two have much in common. Some students aren't comfortable with interpretation, because with interpretation there is no right or wrong "answer." In other words, there is no right or wrong way of "seeing" or interpreting a poem, story, or book.

Like the restaurant review or the movie review, the interpretive essay relies on a set of criteria that is established by the writer of the paper. These criteria are based on the writer's value system, perceptions about the world, and observations of relationships.

A writer's set of criteria is based on the feelings and past experiences of the writer. The writer responds to the poem, story, or novel and relates its concepts, themes, plot, and characters to his or her own life experiences. Your instructor may refer to this type of interpretation as "reader response."

The most important skills you will need to interpret a piece of literature include the following:

- Reading for comprehension
- Note-taking skills—writing in your book as you read
- Analytical skills—asking what the story *means*
- Organizational skills—deciding how to organize your interpretation

Beginning the Interpretive Essay

After you have read the literary selection chosen for this assignment, answer the following questions:

1. Write a paragraph in which you identify the characters and their roles. What motivates each character?

2. Highlight repeated ideas in your text. Then think about the text as a whole. Is there a reason that the writer keeps referring to a certain object or concept? What is the writer trying to communicate by making these repetitions?

3. Write several sentences in which you comment on the form of the story. Why are events ordered in this way? What can you say about the author's tone and persona in the story?

4. Think about how this story fits into American culture today. What problems do we have that are addressed by this story?

5. Summarize the story in a paragraph.

6. Describe the main character's perspective. What is the situation, and how does he or she deal with the events in the story?

7. Explain your ideas about the theme (the main idea) of this story.

Interpretive Thesis Statement

Look at the paragraphs you have written. Choose the two that were the most interesting and think of questions these paragraphs present; then decide which concepts you will analyze and interpret in your essay.

Here are a few questions that may help you come up with a focus for your interpretation:

• How does the plot mirror events in my own life? What can I learn about life, relationships, or human nature from these parallels?

• What can this story tell me about my own attitudes and beliefs? Which of my beliefs were challenged by this story? Which beliefs were affirmed? What issues did this story make me consider in a different light, and why?

• Who was the main character, and what motivated this character? How did the character interact with other characters? What can this character's motivations and actions tell a reader about human nature and/or human relationships?

• What recurring symbols or metaphors have you identified? How do these symbols and/or metaphors create a separate layer of meaning?

After you have decided on a possible focus for your essay, write out your idea as a complete sentence. The sentence should include the title of the piece of literature you are interpreting, its author, and the primary focus of your essay. This is a thesis statement. Exchange your thesis idea with some of your classmates. Look at your group's ideas, and comment on them in group discussion. After discussion, revise your thesis according to your group's suggestions and your own feelings. Remember that even if your thesis is quite similar to that of a classmate, you probably will be writing very different essays.

Writing the Interpretive Essay

Interpretive essays are similar to, but not the same as, review essays. In an interpretive essay, you try to persuade the audience to share your ideas, or interpretations, of different aspects of what you are interpreting (in this case, a story). Your thesis statement should indicate the title and author of the story, what aspects of the story you are interpreting, and how you are interpreting those aspects.

The most common (and fatal) error that students make in writing this essay is including too much summarization of the story. Go further than that—explain how and why we as readers should interpret the story in the same way you did.

After you have written your thesis statement, you should think of three or four main points you can make to support the thesis. Write them out in an outline.

When you have made your outline and written out your main points in complete sentences, go through the text of the story. Find no more than four quotes from the story that you can use to explain and illustrate your points. You can also use paraphrase and summary to illustrate your points, but as mentioned above, use summary in tasteful amounts. Illustrative quotes, paraphrases, and summaries should not be more than two typed lines long. You may also use outside sources, but do not over-rely on these sources. Make your own points, and use the sources to back up those points (not the other way around).

The important thing to remember while writing is that *any* interpretation is valid as long as you can back it up with logic, illustrations, and examples.

Now that you have completed an outline and gathered your illustrations, it's time to write the rough draft. Don't worry so much about the introduction and conclusion yet; just write down your thesis statement at the beginning and at the end so that your group will be able to figure out what you're writing about.

Rough Draft Peer Edit, Interpretive Essay

As a group, decide whose essay you will do first; answer these questions about that person's essay, then the next person's, and so on.

1. Read over the whole draft. Is there a unifying idea, or does the writer seem to be a little disorganized? Find the unifying idea and write it out in a sentence to group discussion.

2. Look for transitions between paragraphs. Counsel the writer if more transitions are needed between ideas to create a "flow" of ideas.

3. Read each paragraph carefully. Each paragraph should contain a topic sentence which explains the interpretive idea or criteria, defines it, and gives examples from the text of the story (or another source, if applicable). If any of these elements are missing in any of the paragraphs, mention this in group discussion.

4. Finally, give the writer ideas for an introduction and conclusion. Look at the thesis statement. Does it match the body of the essay, or has the writer gone off the thesis? Suggest thesis statement revisions. Think of the ideas and explanations that need to occur in the introduction so that the essay is readable and interesting.

Second Draft Peer Edit, Interpretive Essay

1. Read your partner's draft carefully, circling parts where you don't understand his or her meaning.

2. Go through the draft and cross out all instances of "I believe," "In my opinion," and "I think"; the essay is interpretive, so we know that the writer thinks and believes what he or she is writing. Also cross out all instances of "you" and "your" unless they appear in direct quotes.

3. Proofread for correct citation, making sure that the writer has put all direct quotes in quotation marks and has identified paraphrases and summaries from the story.

4. Check for references to the author; make sure the writer is referring to the author by his or her last name or first and last name. Never refer to an author only by his or her first name.

5. Proofread for pronoun problems. Every pronoun should refer to a word that precedes it (an antecedent) in the sentence itself or in a previous sentence. If you need to review what pronouns are, use your handbook.

6. Look for transitions between paragraphs. Has the writer adequately strung the parts of the essay together, or does it read like a bunch of paragraphs thrown down at random? Help the writer smooth out the essay so that it is "seamless."

7. Think about the writer's tone in the essay. Has he or she kept a consistent persona throughout the essay? Are there random slang words or digressions in tone? Mark any problem areas.

8. No summary of the story should be more than two typed lines long. If you find an area of the essay that contains too much summary, mark it.

9. Does the writer provide adequate topic sentences (with explanations of value judgments), good illustrations and examples from the

text, and proper quote introductions? If not, mark the areas that need work.

10. Proofread the entire essay for run-on sentences, fragments, misused words, and errors in grammar, punctuation, and spelling.

Student Example: The Interpretive Essay

The Power of Love
Shruthi Manjunath

The story "Love Medicine" (1982) by Louise Erdrich is about the life of a young Native American, Lipsha, who lives on a reservation. Lipsha's grandma has taken care of him since he was young, and now that he has grown up, it's his turn to take care of his grandpa. The story tells us of Lulu Lamartine, who was a friend of grandpa's in childhood and has had a crush on him ever since. In the story, the narrator, Lipsha, has some sort of magical, mysterious power called "the touch." Using this touch, Lipsha can cure people of their ailments. That's why, Lipsha, although a failure at his studies, is quite a hero among the people of his reservation.

"Love Medicine" is a short story that is set on a Native American reservation. People here are still mostly uneducated and quite rural. The story takes place at a time when people have a strong belief in superstition and magic, and they believe in Lipsha's "touch."

Lipsha, the narrator, takes us through the life of his grandparents. Grandpa, now very old, is a little unstable and needs somebody to take care of him. However, he is after another woman, Lulu Lamartine. This has his wife very angry with him and she wants Lipsha to put the touch on grandpa, to cure him. Lipsha then tries to cure Grandpa and along the way realizes some new things about life.

Lipsha is uneducated and naïve in his view of life. In the beginning he says, "I never really done much with my life, I suppose. I never had a television." He feels that getting a job and earning money and buying things is all there is to life.

He sees his grandma crying and mourning for her husband, and this touches him. He talks about how he thought love died down as people grew older, but here he saw it rear up like a whip and lash. This is an example of beautiful imagery. It describes how he realized what love was, and it could also imply that the whip has hit him and awakened him to his senses. As he says later, he probably will go out and find that woman whom he could love and share his life with.

Lipsha makes observations that on the face look meaningless and sometimes even silly. But when we think about them, the real truth in them shows. Modernization has made us numb and cold to life's real meaning. He talks about God going deaf and not hearing our prayers. He suggests that people aren't speaking God's language anymore. This is the real truth. Isn't it true that we are hardening up inside and becoming insensitive to everybody around us? We are so caught up in pursuing the riches that we have forgotten the meaning of life. We've forgotten how lucky we are to be alive today. We've forgotten why God sent us down here. We've forgotten what it is like to be one with the animals and birds that God made for us. And we've forgotten what it is like to be human. Lipsha has never been to school and we can see this in the way he thinks. And it makes me wonder if going to school, getting educated, and getting a good job is the best thing we ought to do. He is also so naïve that even though he makes us think our lives, it is not very clear if he has realized this truth himself. He is still wondering, "Even now I have to wonder if Higher Power turned it back, if we got to yell, or if we just don't speak its language."

In "Love Medicine," the grandpa is quite immature. He is very old but still does not realize his position and duty in life. Grandpas are supposed to be sweet, old people who tell stories to the kids and look after them. You see, in my home country of India, even though the grandpa is the oldest he still has some form of control on the family. He is involved in making the big decisions of the house—for example, buying a new house. I, coming from a traditional Asian background, find it somewhat strange that grandpa is still running after women. Grandpas are the wisest in the family, and they are the ones who guide the children as they go along. They are also the ones who are respected the most due to their long experience in life. However, here I find an entirely different kind of grandpa, one who doesn't care for his wife's feelings and doesn't seem to be concerned about his only grandson.

The story, nevertheless, tells us that love is what finally counts in life. Whether it is love for your wife, children, or life itself. The touch that is described in the story is also, I feel, an extension of real love. Lipsha was the kind of person who knew the meaning and power of love. He was one who could give away love to anybody who asked for it. And he knew how to listen to people and their problems, and he "cured" them by simply giving them a part of his love. In the beginning, when he describes how he cured his grandma's aching legs, he is simply listening to her and showing his concern and love for her. What he describes as snapping the knots of veins in her legs, is actually massaging her legs. This is a very common, everyday thing in India. The son or daughter usually sits by the bedside and massages the grandma or grandpa's legs so that they can go to sleep without any pain. Lipsha was doing the same thing.

Thus the story "Love Medicine" tells us about the power of love. It wants us to understand that love is the ultimate emotion and it comes only from the heart. No outside medicine or trick or magic is going to make it work. As Lipsha himself puts it, "So what I'm heading at is this. I finally convinced myself that the real actual power to the love medicine was not the goose heart itself but the faith in the cure." Love is the same all over the world because it comes from the heart. The touch that is described in the story is really a symbol of love, and to make the love medicine work you've got to believe in it first. And I think today's fast life and competition is making us blind and numb to life's real treasure: love.

4

The Argument/Research Essay

Argument/Research Essay Overview

Writing an effective research essay that puts forth an argument requires almost all the skills you have learned in the previous essays, plus a few new ones. For instance, you will need to define and describe, which you learned in the narrative essay; you will need to employ several strategies of development, which you learned in the explanatory essay; you will need to evaluate your sources and make judgments about where to include them in your paper, a skill you learned in your evaluative essays; additionally, you will be learning how to construct an effective argument and complete necessary research.

The main idea of an argument essay is not to "argue" in the sense that most people think of the word. Most people think of arguments as emotionally charged confrontations, but emotions have very little to do with an effective academic argument, which is more like an intellectual debate or discussion about a topic. In an argument essay, you will present your point of view on a controversial subject and provide evidence that your point of view has more merit than competing points of view. You will gain this evidence through research in the library and on the World Wide Web/Internet.

Rogerian Argument

Carl Rogers, a respected psychotherapist, researcher, counselor, and teacher, put forth this theory of communication: ". . . the major barrier to mutual interpersonal communication is our very natural tendency to judge, to evaluate, to approve or disapprove, the statement of the other person, or the other group" (330). Think about the last disagreement or argument you participated in or witnessed. We can't disagree with someone unless we evaluate his or her opinion, reasons for holding an opinion, and/or the ramifications of holding such an opinion. By nature, human beings tend to judge one another on physical appearance, expressions of emotions, and expressions of thoughts (verbal and non-verbal). Many of us make heroic efforts *not* to judge one another, but judging is often an unconscious, reflexive act.

Rogers postulates that the only way to overcome this barrier of judgment is to "listen with understanding" (331). This type of listening goes beyond our ordinary habits. It involves not only hearing a person's reasons for holding an opinion, but delving into the logic behind these opinions and the life experiences that formed these opinions until we have an empathic understanding of the person and his or her beliefs. Rogers suggests this exercise:

> The next time you get into an argument with your [spouse], or your friend, or with a small group of friends, just stop the discussion for a moment and for an experiment, institute this rule. "Each person can speak up for himself only *after* he has first restated the ideas and feelings of the previous speaker accurately, and to that speaker's satisfaction." You see what this would mean. It would simply mean that before presenting your own point of view, it would be necessary for you to really achieve the other speaker's frame of reference—to understand his thoughts and feelings so well that you could summarize them for him. . . . once you have been able to see the other's point of view, your own comments will have to be drastically revised. You will also find the emotion going out of the discussion, the differences being reduced, and those differences which remain being of a rational and understandable sort. (332–333)

This is the idea we will use when writing the argument paper. We will strive to understand our opposition's opinions *and* their reasons for holding such opinions. We will state those opinions in the paper as cons, and then either compromise with the opposition's points or refute those points.*

We're getting a little ahead of ourselves, however; the first step in writing an academic argument is choosing a good topic.

---

*For more information on Carl Rogers's theories regarding communication, please consult the publication cited in this section:

Rogers, Carl. "Dealing With Breakdowns in Communication—Interpersonal and Intergroup." *On Becoming a Person.* Boston: Houghton Mifflin, 1961.

Beginning the Argument/Research Essay

Choosing a Topic

The two most common mistakes students make when choosing topics are (1) choosing a topic that really isn't arguable and (2) choosing a topic that they feel too strongly about. Choosing a topic that really isn't arguable is usually an attempt to take the easy way out, because obviously there is a lot of source material out there on the only popular or reasonable point of view. The position, "child abuse is wrong," for example, is not arguable. Who would argue that "child abuse is the right thing to do"? In order for a position to be arguable, you should be able to think of an opposite or contrasting statement that at least one person you know would support.

Choosing a topic that you feel too strongly about is usually a mistake because you will tend to ignore evidence from the other side of the argument. As you will read later, presenting the other side of the argument is actually just as important as presenting your own side.

For help in choosing a topic, answer the following questions:

1. What other classes are you enrolled in this semester? Do you have an essay assignment in any of these classes that could "double" for this assignment? (Remember, this essay has to be *argumentative*, not informative; but you may be able to find research that supports both purposes.)

2. What is your major, or what do you plan to major in? What are some issues in your chosen major or future profession that you would like to research? (Again, remember that the essay is argumentative.)

3. What kind of music do you listen to? Can you recall any controversies surrounding this music?

4. What sports do you enjoy participating in or watching? What controversies about that sport can you recall? What are new trends or rules in this sport?

5. Think about your experiences with elementary and high school education. Was there ever a time that you thought a policy, law, or action was wrong or inappropriate? How could you argue that point?

6. Think about your experiences at college. Again, are there any policies, laws, or actions that you disagree with? How could you argue that point?

7. Do you have children, or are you close to a relative's or friend's child? What issues that concern children interest you?

8. What environmental issues, local or global, interest you?

9. What hobbies or talents do you pursue in your spare time? What hobbies or interests have you abandoned? What are some issues involved in your hobbies that could be termed controversial?

10. What are some of the political or social issues you have heard about on the news? Which of these sounds interesting to research?

11. What issues involving the computer have cropped up in the past few years? Which controversies interest you?

12. What opinions do you have about the criminal justice system (police, courts, etc.)? Can you think of any controversies that you could research on this topic?

13. Think about members of your family who have had health problems. What issues or concerns did you or your family consider while that family member was ill?

14. Think back to the last disagreement you had with someone over an issue. What was the controversy you were discussing? Would you want to research this controversy?

15. What governmental controversies can you think of? Which would you like to research?

16. Go to the library and look at a recent news magazine, like *Time* or *Newsweek*, and write down any interesting issues that are covered. An alternative to this activity is to listen to a public radio news broadcast, visit a news-oriented Web site, or watch the news on television.

Look at the answers to the questions above, and choose three of your favorites from the list. Then complete the following for each:

- Make up a statement involving your topic that has the words "should" or "should not" in it.
- What problems or challenges have you personally encountered with this topic?
- What national or local issues have surrounded this topic?
- What ongoing issues or problems surround this topic? Think of an alternative or off-beat solution to these problems.

Using the answers to the activity above, formulate an argumentative thesis statement.

Thesis Statement Workshop

Get into a group with some classmates, and complete the following activity.

You will score each thesis statement based on this test:

- Check each thesis statement for "arguability"; to do this, read the statement and then formulate an "anti-thesis" (the direct opposition's "thesis statement" that would reply to this thesis statement). If you cannot formulate an "anti-thesis" or if the "anti-thesis" sounds ridiculous (i.e., very few people would agree with that opinion), then the thesis is either not argumentative or really takes no stand (e.g., "Child abuse is wrong.") Give the writer one point if the thesis is arguable and takes a stand. Give the writer zero points if it isn't arguable or doesn't take a stand.
- Check each thesis for narrowness and specifics. If there are words like "good" or "bad," are they defined? Has the writer narrowed the thesis to one specific issue instead of a group of issues? The thesis is probably too broad if an entire book has been written on the subject. Give the writer one point if the thesis is narrow enough.
- Think about audience appeal. Which of the theses appeals to you the most? Why? Give the writer one point if you would like to read an essay based on that thesis statement.

Now tally up the points for each thesis, and decide which one is the most arguable and the most appealing to your group members. You will probably need to revise your thesis statement; ask your group members for their ideas on how best to revise your thesis.

Narrowing Thesis and Pros/Cons

The argumentative research essay must present *both* sides of the issue you are writing about. In your essay, you will present the opposition's points (cons) first, and explain why the opposition's points are wrong (this is called *refuting* the opposition's points). After you have refuted the opposition's points, you present your supporting points (pros) and provide adequate factual support for your claims. As in football, you have to break down the other side's defense before you can complete a touchdown.

In an argumentative essay, the hardest and most important parts of writing the essay happen before you even begin the actual drafting. Without a solid, narrow thesis statement that commits to one side of the issue, your essay will fail; without good pros and cons, your essay will fall flat. The following exercise will help you develop a stronger thesis statement and some good pros and cons.

Activity 1: Narrowing the Thesis   Read your thesis to a group of your classmates. Then listen to your group members' theses. Ask these questions and see if the writer has adequately answered them:

- Who specifically will this issue/thesis affect? In what way?
- Why is this issue/thesis important?
- What specific proposal is this thesis arguing?
- What geographical area is this thesis limited to? (Hint: "the planet" is not narrow enough.)
- What time frame does this thesis imply or specifically state?
- Is this thesis arguing a solution to a problem or an alternate viewpoint on an existing problem? Is it clear?

While you are working, take a look at what other people are asking you. Then revise your thesis so that it is narrower and easier to understand.

Activity 2: Developing Pros and Cons   Look over your group members' theses, and offer suggestions on pros, cons, supporters, and opposers. If you have questions about your own pros and cons, talk these questions over with classmates and/or your instructor. Remember that supporters and opposers can be local; you are free to interview local authorities on the subjects you write about. After about thirty minutes of discussion, stop, collect the information, and begin writing your pros, cons, and lists of supporters and opposers. You should have three pros, three cons, three supporters, and three opposing individuals or organizations.

Remember that your pros and cons *should not* be reflective. This means that your pros shouldn't be answers to your cons. They should stand by themselves. For example:

Thesis statement: Gambling casinos should be allowed in every Iowa county.

Right:
Pro: Gambling creates much-needed revenues for Iowa government.
Con: Iowans are more likely to become gambling addicts with casinos so close by.

Wrong:
Pro: There is no proof that casinos cause gambling addiction.
Con: Iowans are more likely to become gambling addicts with casinos so close by.

In the second example, the pro reflects or argues with the con. This isn't really a pro, it is a *refutation* of the con. You need refutations, but they shouldn't be listed as pros.

Peer Checklist: Preliminary Research Plans

Get into groups of three or four and discuss the following questions regarding everyone's topic. Write down comments or information you get from other group members, and then fill in the blanks with your own ideas/opinions after class.

1. Tell the group what your tentative thesis is and why you chose it.

2. Ask other group members what they know about the issue. How old is this issue? What has happened in recent or not-so-recent history concerning this issue? What are the social implications of this issue? What are the political effects of this issue? Has this issue affected anyone's philosophies or ideas? What experiences have group members had with this issue?

3. Ask the group for arguments that support your thesis (pros).

4. Ask the group if they know of any individuals or groups that would support your thesis.

5. Ask the group for arguments against your thesis (cons).

6. Ask the group if they know of any individuals or groups that would oppose your thesis.

After brainstorming with your group, use the answers you have gathered to do preliminary research for your preliminary outline. *Preliminary research* means devoting an hour or two to library and/or Web searches to find the pros (points that support your thesis) and the cons (points that oppose your thesis).

It is much easier to find pros and cons if you can identify groups or individuals who support or oppose your thesis. That is the goal of preliminary research.

After you've done your preliminary research and found at least three pros and at least three cons, begin your preliminary outline.

Searching the Library

There are a few important things to remember when searching the library, to ensure that you are searching the right files for the right information.

1. DO be aware of exactly what you are looking for. What's your topic? What information do you need? Write out a specific thesis statement that you can use to search for materials. For example, if you are looking for an article on what kinds of cosmetics are tested on animals and how the animals are treated during the experiments, your research questions may read like this: "Which cosmetic companies test on animals? What kinds of tests are done? What groups oppose animal testing?" These questions will yield more results than a vague statement, such as: "My essay is about testing on animals."

2. DO be aware of how important current information is on your topic. If you are researching history, you may think that it is unimportant if your information is twenty years old; however, you also may be missing out on a new development, new perspective, or new knowledge.

3. DON'T search just one database! Most libraries have functions to search books, videos, journals, magazines, and other periodicals. KNOW which database you are searching in and how commands work in each. Also, you can often search libraries around the world right from your terminal. If you have a tricky subject, sometimes these databases can come in handy; but remember, it takes some time for distant libraries to send materials to your home library, so order your interlibrary loan books early.

4. DON'T always search by subject. Try the keyword function to find more articles or books that mention your topic in the abstract (the explanation underneath the book or article entry).

5. DON'T try just one keyword or subject search for your topic and then give up. Be creative; think of synonyms for your keyword or subject and try searching them too. The excuse, "They didn't have anything on my topic," is rarely founded. It just means you gave up too soon.

6. DO print out the entries you think you will use. It will help you and/or the librarian find your sources more quickly.

7. DO photocopy or print out anything you can, instead of checking it out. It's easy to forget to take back your books, and you'll end up with a nasty overdue charge!

8. DO be careful with your computer diskette at the library. Don't stand in the magnetic stream or leave your book bag near it for a long period of time; it will erase your diskette. NEVER set your diskette down anywhere near the book desensitizer. It is a very powerful magnet and will erase your files almost immediately.

Internet Search Tips

When searching the Internet for source material, it is very important to search *specifically* and to search *reputable sources.*

Do's and Don'ts of Internet Searching

1. DO use a search engine that searches multiple kinds of Web pages. When possible, do an advanced or boolean search (review the detailed explanation of boolean searching in the explanatory paper chapter). Most search engines have detailed instructions on how to complete very specific searches. Click on the "help" or "search tips" icon.

2. DON'T use general terms like "music" when you're really looking for information on music written by Tori Amos. String related words together (they don't have to make sense or be a complete sentence). A good string for the search above would be "Tori Amos" AND "music" AND "composer." By making your searches specific, you will more likely run across the exact Web site you're looking for.

3. DO read over all the "hits" on the page before "surfing" to the first site that looks interesting.

4. DO print out interesting pages, noting the http: address in the location window. You will need this address for your Works Cited page.

5. DO bookmark sites that you would like to return to or that you are certain you will use.

6. DON'T use pages that are purely one person's opinion, unless that person backs up their statements with sources or is reputable in the field. Beware of pages that are selling products; these pages are not often good source material on anything but their products and their prices.

7. DO use links and ideas from a good Web page. Another option is to contact the page's author(s) and ask for additional information. Most Web page authors list their e-mail address at the bottom of the page. Just click on it and write!

Writing Preliminary Outlines

Before you begin your actual research, you should draw up a preliminary outline that indicates, in complete sentences, your thesis statement, the opposition's points (cons), and the supporter's points (pros). Remember to indicate in each con that the opposition to your thesis believes the cons (see the underlined phrases below); otherwise, it may sound as if you're arguing with yourself. Here's an example:

    I. Introduction
    Thesis statement:
    Cigarette companies should be considered legally responsible for the lung cancer deaths of lifetime smokers.

II. First opposing point:

Those who argue that cigarette companies should not be legally liable for the deaths of smokers argue that smoking is a personal choice and was not forced upon these people; therefore their deaths are their own responsibility.

III. Second opposing point:

Another point of those opposed to holding cigarette companies liable for smoking-related deaths is that the tobacco industry is necessary to a viable American economy; if lawsuits are filed by all families of lung cancer victims, cigarette companies will go out of business and leave our economy in a shambles.

IV. Third opposing point:

Lung cancer also occurs among the nonsmoking population and is the result of many factors, not just smoking; therefore, the companies should not be liable, according to cigarette company supporters.

V. First supporting point:

Cigarette companies have increased the addictive amounts of nicotine in cigarettes for the sole purpose of "hooking" smokers.

VI. Second supporting point:

Cigarette companies advertise to children and teenagers with the intent of "hooking" teenagers on cigarettes and making them lifetime smokers.

VII. Third supporting point:

Cigarette companies have studied nicotine and other aspects of cigarettes for many years and have misrepresented the dangers of smoking to the public.

VIII. Conclusion

Thesis statement:

Cigarette companies should be considered legally responsible for the lung cancer deaths of lifetime smokers.

After you have written your preliminary outline, go to the library and/or the Web and begin searching for sources that back up your assertions (both your pros and cons).

Workshop

Get into groups of three or four. Then read through others' thesis statements, pros and cons, commenting on the following:

1. Is the thesis narrow enough for the page limit?

2. Do the pros or cons have the words "good" or "bad" or other words that imply value judgments (such as "menace," "harmful," "helpful," etc.) without defining exactly what is meant by "good" or "bad"? These words must be defined so that the statements make sense.

3. Are all the points supportable? Do you think research is available to support each point? Do you have suggestions for the writer as to where he or she might find research, a person to interview, or other source of information?

4. Are the cons refutable? Do you think there is research available that will refute each con? Do you have suggestions for the writer as to where he or she might find research, a person to interview, or other source of information?

Finishing Your Outline

When you have completed your research and read through your sources, complete your outline. Here's a revised version of our first example, complete with refutations. *Refutations* are the part of the argument that proves the cons wrong and/or compromises with the cons. After reading your sources, you will be able to get a better idea of which refutations are supportable.

I. Introduction

Thesis statement:

Cigarette companies should be considered legally responsible for the lung cancer deaths of lifetime smokers.

II. First opposing point:

Those who argue that cigarette companies should not be legally liable for the deaths of smokers argue that smoking is a personal choice and was not forced upon these people; therefore their deaths are their own responsibility.

Refutation (compromise): While some people smoke despite knowing the risks involved, many people who smoke have been led to believe, through deceptive advertising, that smoking is not a health risk.

III. Second opposing point:

Another point of those opposed to holding cigarette companies liable for smoking-related deaths is that the tobacco industry is necessary to a viable American economy; if lawsuits are filed by all families of lung cancer victims, cigarette companies will go out of business and leave our economy in a shambles.

Refutation: While it is true that the ruination of tobacco companies would adversely affect the economy, this fact has nothing to do with the issue of legal responsibility.

IV. Third opposing point:

Lung cancer also occurs among the nonsmoking population and is the result of many factors, not just smoking; therefore, the companies should not be liable, according to cigarette company supporters.

Refutation (compromise): While it is true that lung cancer occurs in the nonsmoking population, numerous studies have proven a definite link between heavy smoking and lung cancer.

V. First supporting point:

Cigarette companies have increased the addictive amounts of nicotine in cigarettes for the sole purpose of "hooking" smokers.

VI. Second supporting point:

Cigarette companies advertise to children and teenagers with the intent of "hooking" teenagers on cigarettes and making them lifetime smokers.

VII. Third supporting point:

Cigarette companies have studied nicotine and other aspects of cigarettes for many years and have misrepresented the dangers of smoking to the public.

VIII. Conclusion

Thesis statement:

Cigarette companies should be considered legally responsible for the lung cancer deaths of lifetime smokers.

Researching Effectively

Chances are that after you have completed your first round of research, you will find that you need additional sources for your refutations. There are several shortcuts to finding good sources:

• Look at a source you have already found, and check for a bibliography or a list of Works Cited. If the source lists its own sources, you have the opportunity to read these sources for yourself, and use parts the author of the original source did not use. However, you should not use *only* the sources you find in another author's Works Cited or bibliography. You aren't writing the same essay, after all!

• Many authors, especially those who write about issues in their field, write numerous articles on the same issue. Search both the Web and the library for additional articles and books by that author. However, do not rely on only one or two authors for all your source material; try to balance your essay with multiple sources by a variety of authors.

   • Look through your sources for repeated phrases or words. Do searches on these phrases and words on the Web and in the library.

   • If printed sources are in short supply on your topic, consider interviewing local authorities on the subject.

MLA Style Basics

MLA style is a system designed to assist students and teachers with citing sources (giving credit to an author for a quote or idea). While most students know that they need to give an author credit for a direct quote ["To be or not to be" (Shakespeare)], many students do not know that they need to give an author credit for a paraphrased idea [Hamlet thinks about whether he should live or die (Shakespeare)].

   MLA style is different from footnoting. Actually, using MLA style is much easier. Instead of worrying about having enough room at the bottom of a page for footnotes, a writer simply types the citation right in the text. See the fictitious example below:

Angie's thesis statement is:
Breast cancer should be allocated as much government funding as heart disease.

Angie read an article in *Healthy Woman* magazine about this issue and decided to use some facts and statistics from the article in her essay. This is how it will appear on her Works Cited page (attached at the end of her essay).

> Baratono, Michelle. "Men's Health Concerns Are Monopolizing Government Funding." *Healthy Woman.* February 28, 1994: 56–60.

In her paper, Angie quotes the article directly; notice how she adequately prepares the reader for the quote by indicating why the quote supports her point:

> American women are among the most privileged in the world. In America, a woman can hold the same job as almost any man; she can hold public office; she can fight for her rights and win. However, American women are fighting a life or death battle right now against an enemy growing in strength—breast cancer: "One in every ten women in the United States will develop this dreaded disease, and the numbers are increasing" (Baratono 57).

Later in her paper, Angie paraphrases the article. This is how paraphrasing should look:

> Several women have taken their concerns to their congressional representatives, demanding that breast cancer be funded to the extent that heart disease and diabetes are funded. So far, their demands have fallen on deaf ears (Baratono 59).

If the author's name appears in your quote introduction or paraphrase, you don't need to include it in the citation (here's a paraphrased example):

> Baratono asserts that breast cancer is every woman's nightmare (60).

Beginning the Bibliography or Works Cited

It is important to begin your Works Cited page as soon as you have gathered some sources together for your essay. Directions for writing entries for books, magazine articles, electronic sources (databases, Web pages, etc.) are available in most handbooks, both in print and online.

Using Reputable Sources

To make sure you have a source that is reputable and usable, answer the questions below (there are separate sections for Web sources and library sources).

The reason you should evaluate your sources is simple: You want good, reliable information. If you can't identify the author of a source or a Web page, it's probably not a good source; after all, someone didn't even want to put his or her name on it, and you don't know what those person's credentials are, if they have any at all. On the other hand, an article written by someone educated in your topic or someone who has had direct experience with your topic is both credible and interesting. *Don't always believe everything you see in print; make sure the truth is being represented in a fair manner.*

Analyze your sources based on the following questions.

Library Sources

1. What is the author's name and his or her credentials for writing on this topic?

2. Who are the authorities on the subject that are interviewed or quoted in the article/book?

3. What statistics related to your topic are contained in the source? Who sponsored the studies—a biased or unbiased group?

4. Where and by whom was the book/magazine published? What agenda does this organization ascribe to that could have affected the slant of the book/magazine?

5. What year was this book/magazine published? If it is more than five years old, what evidence do you have that the information included in the publication is still valid?

Web Sources

1. Who is the author of the Web page? What credentials does this person possess on this topic?

2. What organization sponsors the Web page? What agenda does this organization ascribe to that could affect the slant and material included in the Web page?

3. If statistics are used, is the source of the statistics referred to? If so, is it unbiased and credible?

4. Does the Web page quote authorities on the subject? Who are they and what are their credentials?

5. What is the tone of the Web page? Does it sound juvenile? Are words misspelled? Is the grammar sloppy?

6. When was the Web page published (this info is at the bottom of most pages)? Is the information still valid?

Bibliography/Source Evaluation Workshop

Print out your Works Cited page and give it to a classmate. Then complete the following activity on your partner's bibliography.

Using the information your partner has provided on his or her bibliography, look up and find the sources he or she has listed. Here are some hints:

For books and magazines, get into the right library database and do an author search.

For Web pages, type the http: address in the location window. If this doesn't work, get into a search engine and search for the title or author's name (use quotation marks to group words or names together).

1. For the Web pages, books, and magazines that you find, check the information included in the page or library entry. If any information does not match the information in the bibliography, edit the bibliography.

2. Mark the bibliography entries you were unable to find. If you know why you were unable to find the entries, include a note about what information needs to be included in the entries.

3. Check the bibliography for MLA style. If it is incorrect, make a note to the writer (you do not have to correct the mistakes, just point them out—the writer is responsible for fixing errors).

Types of Evidence

Your sources will contain various kinds of evidence. You should seek to strike a balance between the types of evidence you use in your paper so that your paper is balanced, well focused, and well researched.

Empirical evidence (facts):   Logical facts, such as study results (percentages, statistics, etc.), are usually fairly reliable as evidence. Make sure you note who sponsored the studies you are citing, however, as some studies find what they are paid to find. It would be no surprise, for example, to find that the National Rifle Association's statistics on gun-related deaths in the United States are significantly lower than the same statistics furnished by the United States government. Know the bias of your sources.

Personal testimony: Evidence provided by a person who has first-hand experience with your topic is often valuable, though sometimes slanted. Analyze the person's testimony and learn something about his or her background before deciding to use his or her testimony to back your points.

Authoritative testimony: Evidence provided by an esteemed authority on the subject is often valuable; experts are usually educated in the area in which they are providing their opinion. Again, check their credentials and connections to find biases.

Inference: Coming to a conclusion based on observation is also a way of gathering evidence. Inferences can be gleaned from one's personal experience, other sources, or both. Analyzing one's own biases, though often difficult, is necessary if one is going to use inference.

Review Activity: MLA Style

We learned how to quote, paraphrase, and summarize using MLA style in the Explanatory Essay chapter. This exercise will help you review what you learned about running acknowledgements and Works Cited entries. Use one of your sources to answer the questions.

1. Choose a direct quote and write a running acknowledgment in the middle of the quotation sentence.

2. Choose a direct quote and write a running acknowledgment in the beginning of the quotation sentence.

3. Choose a direct quote and write a running acknowledgment at the end of the quotation sentence (see handout, page 211).

4. Choose a direct quote and leave out extraneous parts of the quotation sentence.

5. Choose a short section and paraphrase it, using a simple paraphrase.

6. Choose a short section and paraphrase it, using a running acknowledgment.

7. Choose a short section and paraphrase it, directly quoting one or two terms or short phrases.

8. Choose a short section and paraphrase it with an introductory running acknowledgment.

9. Summarize the longest section.

10. Write a Works Cited entry for the source, using your handbook as a guide.

Completing your Works Cited page now will assist you in the next stage of drafting.

Gathering Evidence and Inserting It

Activity 1   Show your current outline to the group. Look at others' outlines. How can they be changed so that the points appear to be in the correct order? What is the strongest pro? The weakest con? Talk it over and help each other make revisions to your outlines.

Activity 2   When you have finished discussing possible changes in your outlines, make revisions you deem necessary. Then go over your sources and think about what kinds of evidence you have found to support both your own points and explain the opposition's points (you should use more than one type of evidence in your essay). Start filling out your outline, incorporating notes as to what quotes, summaries, and paraphrases you will use. (Hint: It's easier to write your essay later if you do this in MLA style—see examples below.)

II. First con: Tobacco companies claim that cigarettes do not
                 cause cancer.
                 facts: Marlboro tobacco study results (Roberts 10–12)
                 informed opinion: Tobacco company president's
                 quote (qtd in Brewer 26)

Refutation:
                 inference: six independent studies found cigarettes
                 cause cancer (Wright 34–37), (Peters 87)
                 authoritative testimony: quote from lung cancer
                 specialist, Mayo clinic (qtd in Trotsky 100)

By incorporating your MLA citations right in your outline, you just have
to type them into the body of your essay as you use them, eliminating the
need to look them up repeatedly to make sure you're doing it right.

Writing the Rough Draft

If you have completed all the steps to writing an argumentative essay so
far, now you are ready to write the rough draft. Simply follow your revised outline, inserting your own ideas, explaining the quotes, paraphrases, and summaries you are inserting, and, essentially, making your
argument. Use the Peer Review Checksheets that follow to help you revise your essay.

Argument Essay Rough Draft Peer Checksheet

Complete this worksheet on each of your group members' essays.

Give your draft to someone else in your group. After everyone has
traded, go around the circle and read aloud the draft you were given. As
a group (you may want to assign a person to do each "duty"), listen and
look for the following, commenting or interrupting the reader as necessary (the reader will also have to mark on the essay as he/she reads):

A. *Information and Logic*
        Does the essay present believable, substantiated information and
logic? If not, don't be bashful; speak up and let the writer know where
he or she needs to add more source material to back up his or her allega-
tions, or where he or she needs to rethink the logical flow of the essay.

B. *Flow*
        Is the essay choppy, with no relationship between paragraphs to
clue the reader in to what is coming next? Are some ideas presented in

an odd order, or are ideas widely separated that should have been mentioned at the same time? Renumber the paragraphs if their order seems illogical.

C. *Sources as Crutches*

The writer should be making his or her own points and backing them up with references, much as a lawyer would back up a case with witnesses and evidence. Sources shouldn't be cited in the topic sentences for pros or cons. If the writer is overquoting sources and letting them make entire points for him or her, note this in the essay.

D. *Missing Elements: Definitions, Descriptions, Evidence*

Circle words or ideas the writer needs to explain or define; ask questions about concepts that need description; and look at the types of evidence used in the essay. Has the writer used only one type of evidence (relying only on statistics, for example)? If so, point out other types of evidence the writer could use and where he or she could incorporate them.

E. *Refutations and Compromises*

Check the opposition's points carefully. These paragraphs should appear first in the essay. Each paragraph should be centered on an opposition's point, identifying it as the opposition's point, explaining and defining it, and then refuting or compromising with it. If any of these elements are missing or not clear, mark this on the paper.

F. *Introductions and Conclusions*

Is the introduction just a bland collection of general material? Is the conclusion just a summary of the topic sentences? Suggest ways the writer could write a stronger intro and conclusion.

Workshop Checksheets for Further Drafts

Peer Review Checksheet 1

Read your essay aloud to the group and discuss the following:

1. While listening to the "con" points, or the beginning of the draft, *in each paragraph* make sure the writer has identified the opposition as the opposition, explained its point of view using various types of evidence, and then refuted or compromised with the opposition's point. If any of these steps are missing, discuss how the writer could improve the paragraph.

2. While listening to the "pro" points, *in each paragraph* make sure the writer has identified the point and how it relates to the thesis statement, explained the point and supported it using various types of evidence, and ended on a strong, reinforcing statement. Discuss how the writer could strengthen his or her supporting points.

3. Finally, notice the organization of the essay. Has the writer begun with the weakest con and ended with the strongest pro? Discuss how the order of the essay could be changed to make it stronger.

Trade essays with someone in the group, and complete the following on their draft:

1. Find the topic sentence of each paragraph and underline it. Now look in the paragraph for definitions, descriptions, and explanations of the topic sentence and, more importantly, how the topic sentence relates to the thesis statement. If any of these descriptions, definitions, or explanations is missing, note this fact in the margin.

2. For each con paragraph, evidence should be given that explains the opposition's viewpoint, as well as evidence given to prove the refutation of the opposition's viewpoint. If evidence is scanty, unsupported, or absent, mark this in the margin.

3. In each pro paragraph, evidence should support the writer's topic sentence. If the evidence is scanty, unsupported, or absent, mark this in the margin.

4. Help the writer with the introduction. Think of an introductory strategy that might work well with this topic: a story, a question, a joke, a statistic, or some other innovative opener. Write your ideas on the draft.

5. The first time a source is used, there should be a running acknowledgment that contains the source's author's name and qualifications. If the writer has left out this information, make a note in the margin.

6. Check over the draft for proofing errors and MLA style errors.

7. Cross out all instances of these wishy-washy words: society; I feel; I believe; I think; you; yours; it seems to me; in my opinion; seem; probably; and kind of.

Peer Review Checksheet 2

Answer the following questions about each person's essay, and discuss them (you probably will all want to start with the same essay, so that you are all "talking" about the same things at the same time).

1. Read the whole essay through so you have a sense of how the whole thing is organized. Is the thread of the argument always clear to the reader? An argument should build on itself to come to a solid conclusion. If this isn't happening, often it is because of one of the following:

- The cons aren't identified as cons. Cons should be prefaced with "Those opposing _____ believe" or "Supporters of _____ allege" or a similar indication that someone else, not the writer, believes the con points.
- There are no refutations for the cons.
- There is no transition paragraph from cons/refutations to pros.
- There are inadequate pros, or pros that repeat or parrot refutations.
- Transitions that hold the essay together are absent; there is a "choppy" feeling to the writing.

Point out any problems with the above in the person's essay.

2. Analyze the topic sentences for each paragraph: cons, refutations, and pros. Each should outline a specific, provable point that is supported with evidence gleaned from identified sources. If the points are vague or unsupported, indicate how the writer could improve them.

3. How the writer supports his or her points is just as important as making good, specific, supportable points. Most source material should be paraphrased, not quoted; the writer should quote only when material is short, well written, and to the point. If the writer is overquoting or not using running acknowledgments to introduce his or her sources, point out where he or she should make changes. (Reminder: A running acknowledgment is the writer's introduction to a quote that gives the name and credentials of the author—e.g., "John Smith, a prominent heart surgeon, states that . . . ")

Goals for Revision   Write an introduction that sparks interest (preferably using an introductory strategy outlined in your on-line handbook) and a conclusion that pulls the essay together and concludes your argument.

Peer Review Checksheet 3

1. Read over your partner's essay for logic and sense. Mark any problem areas.

2. Proofread for slang words and phrases, cross out all instances of "you" and "yours," and cross out wishy-washy phrases ("I believe," "It seems to me," "I think," and "I feel"). Notice if the writer is varying his or her running acknowledgments for sources (is the writer always using "John Smith states" or "John Smith writes"?).

3. Look for transitions between paragraphs. Has the writer indicated (through transition words or phrases) how each paragraph is related to the paragraph that came before it? If not, mark, "need transitions," on the paper.

4. Pay particular attention to the point in the essay where the cons end and the pros begin. What could be added to the transitional paragraph to make it clear that a major shift is about to occur?

5. Read the introduction. If it contains entirely general knowledge or bland background material, suggest an introductory strategy to the writer (story, shocking statistic, history, questions, etc.—use your handbook for ideas).

6. Read the conclusion. If it simply parrots the wording of the main points or refutations, it needs to be changed. Are there transitions between ideas in the conclusion, or is it choppy and hard to understand?

7. Check the MLA style. Are paraphrases, quotes, and statistics cited correctly? Remember, in MLA style a parenthetical citation looks like this: (Bigalk 12). The period comes after the citation. Also check the Works Cited. Are they in alphabetical order? Are they written correctly in MLA style?

8. Finally, proofread for errors in grammar, punctuation, and spelling.

Revising Hints   Don't take for granted that your partner or group has found every error in your essay. Look it over yourself, using the checksheets as a guide, and/or go to the writing lab or academic achievement center on your campus and let someone there help you look it over. **Remember that neglecting to cite a paraphrased source correctly is plagiarism; proofread carefully to make sure it is clear which ideas are from source material. Not only the words that belong to an author but his or her *ideas* as well.**

Student Example: Argument Essay

This student began this essay the same way most students do—with no ideas about what topic he would choose, or how he would approach it. By choosing a narrow topic (a specific euthanasia case, rather than the entire topic of euthanasia), Michael succeeded in writing a thought-provoking, sensitive, and effective argument. For practice, you may want to answer the workshop questions above on Michael's essay. Notice the organizational method he uses, and how he uses his sources to support his points.

Kevorkian's Conviction: Death of a Salesman
Michael Badeaux

Mr. Jack Kevorkian, the notorious "Dr. Death," whose direct assistance in the suicides of over 140 people in the last decade has caused considerable controversy, was recently convicted by a lower court in Michigan of second degree murder charges following the most recent suicide in which he assisted. Kevorkian killed Thomas Youk, a Michigan man afflicted with Lou Gehrig's disease, and videotaped the event for broadcast on the weekly news magazine *60 Minutes.* The televising of this broadcast perpetrated a firestorm of criticism and debate, which is what Kevorkian says was his intention in the first place. After standing trial on three separate occasions for assisting in the death of a patient, Kevorkian intended for the law to make a determination about the guilt or innocence of a person that assists in the consensual death of another. Youk's case was different, however. In the past, Kevorkian had allowed the patient to use the "suicide machine" that he had invented, meaning that the patient could simply press a button to end his or her life. In Youk's suicide, however, Kevorkian actively injected him with a series of three drug mixtures to bring about his death and force the Michigan courts to determine whether his brand of euthanasia was legal. Kevorkian has demonstrated his cavalier attitude toward death in both his personal and private life, and his verdict must be upheld as it takes into account both his actions and the man behind those actions, testifying to his self-absorption with death rather than the issue of euthanasia or the relief of suffering for those who turn to him.

Those who oppose Kevorkian's conviction argue that doctors who participate in assisted suicides should not be found guilty of a crime as the patient has given consent to end his or her life, thereby negating any legal repercussions. These proponents of Kevorkian's actions contend that harm must be present for there to be a crime committed. If the individual in question has consented to end his or her life, then no harm is present, and therefore no crime has been committed. The Hemlock Society, the most prominent of the right to die groups, has issued the following statements regarding patient consent and how that consent affects the liability of the physician. "The patient must make a written request signed by two disinterested witnesses. . . . At least one request should be tape recorded and the final request should be video recorded. . . . Criminal sanctions would apply if coercion were proved." Furthermore, Kevorkian's supporters feel that those who assist in ending the suffering of another who wants nothing else but to leave behind their pain and anguish should have their praises sung from the rooftops rather than having criminal charges levied against them. The law, in these people's view, does not have a legal leg to stand on.

The main problem with this belief is that consent is not a legal defense to a criminal act, and the actions of Kevorkian in Youk's case clearly demonstrate the legal requirements of intent and harm. The law takes into account two separate criteria when determining culpability; *mens rea,* or the "evil mind," and *actus reus,* or the "evil deed" (Samaha 78). If an individual breaks a law, his or her intent to break that law must be present, along with the act itself, for concurrence to exist and a crime to have been committed. The harm aspect of Youk's suicide does not occur toward Youk himself or even to his family, but rather to society's trust and support that have been placed in the law and the court's responsibility to uphold the law. As for the issue of consent, the courts have ruled for years that consent is nonbinding in criminal cases.

> While criminal law is designed to protect the interests of society as a whole, the civil law is concerned with enforcing the rights of each individual within the society. So, while the consent of the

victim may relieve the defendant of liability in tort, this same consent has been held irrelevant in a criminal prosecution, where there is more at stake than a victim's rights. . . . To allow an otherwise criminal act to go unpunished because of the victim's consent would not only threaten the security of our society but also might tend to detract from the force of the moral principles underlying the criminal law (Samaha 243, 244).

Although the courts in the United States have debated this issue for years, the consensus seems to give a blunt response to Kevorkian's argument for consent, "The law does not accept that a person can ask to be killed—as Tom Youk clearly did." (Humphry 1).

These statements lay down the law in a literal sense, depicting quite distinctly the status of Kevorkian's legal claims. Judge Jessica Cooper, the presiding judge over Kevorkian's trial, described very succinctly in her closing comments what the errors were in his legal defense of his actions, saying, "You can criticize the law, write or lecture about the law, you can speak to the media or petition the voters, but you must always stay within the limits provided by the law. You may not break the law or take the law into your own hands" (1). Consent is not a legally binding argument in defense of euthanasia, and to claim that it should be binding in the case of patients who have chosen to die is creating an exception to the law that simply cannot be made.

Those who disagree with Kevorkian's conviction argue that Kevorkian himself represents a human example of the euthanasia debate, and that sending him to jail for conducting "mercy killings" sets the euthanasia movement back many years. Derek Humphry, founder of the Hemlock Society, represents this argument in his statement about Kevorkian's conviction, saying "The severity of the sentence on Kevorkian will drive the practice of voluntary euthanasia and assisted suicide even further underground. It will not stop it. Kevorkian is by no means the only doctor who helps people die—just the one who does so

and also openly campaigns for societal acceptance of the practice."
Humphry's position parallels that of other euthanasia supporters who realize that the advancement of their cause has suffered a tremendous set-
back in the eyes of both the courts as well as society at large. This group
has taken Kevorkian under its wing and embraced his actions while giving him an almost god-like status. It had hoped that his efforts would result in further gains for the euthanasia movement as he gave the
American people a point of reference for an otherwise obscure and sel-
dom discussed issue.

The fallacy in this position lies within the man who euthanasia supporters have elected as their savior. Kevorkian has long demonstrated
that he does not take an impartial or neutral view towards death as
physicians must. For this reason, the American Medical Association re-
voked his medical license in 1982, and recently issued a statement in
both defense of their actions as well as condemnation of Kevorkian's
methods. "By invoking the physician-patient relationship to cloak his actions, Jack Kevorkian perverts the idea of the caring and committed
physician, and weakens the public's trust in the medical profession"
(American 1). Some supporters of the euthanasia movement have recog-
nized that Kevorkian went beyond any medical limits when he actively
killed Thomas Youk. George Eighmy, director of an Oregon right to die
group, states, "He brought an issue of the end of life here into our living
rooms, so he must be credited with that. But in his enthusiasm for the
issue he stepped over the line" (qtd. in Sinatra 1). Kevorkian has demonstrated in the past that he takes an almost casual attitude toward assisted suicide, failing to follow any medical guidelines for mental
assessment and competency, and often assisting in suicides for patients
who were not terminally ill. Those who understand medicine and the
place of the physician in regard to the needs of the patient realize that
Kevorkian should not be viewed as a champion of the right to die move-

ment, but rather a charlatan working to satisfy his own fetish behind the mask of euthanasia. His conviction does not set the euthanasia movement back but rather removes a figurehead from the public's view that has clouded its judgement of the issue for over a decade.

Those who oppose this conviction also argue that doctor-assisted suicide represents a highly personal choice for an individual who is confronting the prospects of a long and painful struggle toward death's inevitable outcome. They feel that medicine should be used to bring a painless death to anyone who has lost the will to live. These proponents of the assisted suicide movement argue vehemently that an individual's body belongs solely to that person and cannot be viewed by the law as a piece of property. The individual has complete control of their welfare and must be afforded the right to end their own life should he or she feel inclined to do so. The majority feel that any and all medical options should be pursued to alleviate pain and promote the prolonging of a person's life, but they feel that medicine should also be used if the person feels that he or she does not want to continue forward should their pain and suffering become too great. The mercy aspect of "mercy killing" is the foundation of the euthanasia movement, and it's the guise under which Kevorkian has operated for many years.

This aspect of the euthanasia argument takes it to one of its core issues. Those in support of doctor-assisted suicide argue that medicine should be used to hasten death when the patient wants it and all other medical avenues have been exhausted. Those who oppose this view feel that medicine's role is that of a healer, but once the goal of healing the patient is gone, medicine should be used to lessen pain in allowing death to take its natural course. Kevorkian and his followers are taking the moral low road by ending life rather than making the most of what time that person has left to live. Physicians (as Kevorkian once was) must teach patients to understand death, and how to confront the end of life with understanding and introspection to prepare the mind and heal the soul. New advancements in pain-control therapy an medications allow people to learn how to deal with pain to give them the opportunity to spend their remaining time with friends and loved ones. Kevorkian's option is not one of compassion, but rather one of irresponsibility and haste.

Those supporting Kevorkian's conviction believe that he has not fol-lowed ethical medical practices as only 40 percent of his patients were terminally ill when he assisted in their suicides. The following example of an individual whose suicide he assisted in is but one instance of the over 140 assisted suicides that Kevorkian has taken part in.

> "A single mother of two, Badger had a history of drug and al-cohol abuse, and psychiatric and emotional problems. She was diagnosed with multiple sclerosis but an autopsy found no sign of the disease. Badger, 35, died from a lethal injection. Califor-nia police believe her mother may have encouraged her to seek Kevorkian's help after assisting Badger in two failed sui-cide attempts." (Suicide Machine 1)

The public's perception of Kevorkian's behavior has traditionally been that he assists only those who are terminally ill and have exhausted any and all other medical avenues. The media has promoted this belief throughout the last decade, and is only now starting to report that Kevorkian does not mandate that a patient is suffering from a terminal disease before agreeing to assist him or her with committing suicide. Many of those he assisted in killing could have benefited from other ap-proaches to pain management, and if Kevorkian presupposed to act as their physician, it was his responsibility to bring this point to light before agreeing to assist in ending their lives. He has not done this. This point proves that Kevorkian has shirked his responsibility as a healer and has acted selfishly with little concern for the welfare of these individuals.

Those in favor of Kevorkian's conviction also argue that he neglects to follow any standard medical procedures in determining the mental capacity of those patients who come to him in order to determine if the patient is mentally competent to decide to commit suicide. Many of these individuals came to Kevorkian less than one day prior to their death with Kevorkian at their side. "This is a man who has aided in the deaths of many people whom he did not know and had not previously treated and whose mental competency to decide to die he was in no position to assess" (Trafford 1). The fact that he does not consult with patient's primary care physicians to assess his or her level of competency, and that he does not conduct mental testing to determine what his or her level of awareness is demonstrates great negligence on Kevorkian's part. By failing to assess the mental competency of the individuals that turn to him, Kevorkian once again demonstrates his contempt for medical ethics and the welfare of the patient.

Another argument in favor of Kevorkian's conviction is the fact that these charges and the subsequent conviction take into account the man behind the issue rather than the issue of euthanasia by itself. As Judge Cooper said during the sentencing portion of Kevorkian's trial, "This trial was not about political moral correctness of euthanasia; it was all about you, sir. It was about lawlessness. It was about disrespect for a society that exists and flourishes because of the strength of its legal system. No one, sir, is above the law" (1). Kevorkian has demonstrated a macabre, twisted view toward death throughout his medical career and in his own personal life. He has searched hospital wards in the past looking for patients on the verge of death so that he could conduct research when the moment of death arrived. Rather than allowing the patient to die in peace, he watched like a vulture for the carrion that it hoped to feast upon. Of all the doctors present, only Kevorkian hoped for death. For enjoyment, he paints scenes of beheadings and murder, and has gone so far as to stain one of his paintings with his own blood. In the case of Thomas Youk, Kevorkian became death by killing Youk through a series of injections rather than allowing the patient to commit suicide by use of the death machine that Kevorkian himself developed. This is not the sort of behavior that society intends for its doctors to take. Kevorkian has simply gone too far in his preoccupation with death, and the courts have finally realized that Kevorkian is no more than a rogue whose fetish for death has been allowed to be masked behind the supposedly ethical practice of euthanasia.

Kevorkian's conviction on second degree murder charges does justice to the noble pursuit of medicine. For years he has been allowed to conduct these assisted suicides by finding loopholes in the law, and he has caused great controversy through his actions. This controversy is what he has intended, hoping more to gain public notoriety and satisfy his lust for death than to advance the cause of the euthanasia movement. As a result of his actions, over 140 people have died, most of whom were not afflicted with life-threatening diseases. His actions bring discredit to the medical profession and spit in the face of laws that have been established to guide societal behavior. His own lawyer even dropped him as a client as a direct result of Kevorkian's actions. The jury that put a stop to Kevorkian's work acted in the best interests of the medical profession, the patients that might otherwise turn to him, and of society in general. Their decision should set a precedent for dealing with future "peddlars of death" and will save lives that should not have been lost.

Works Cited

American Medical Association. "The AMA's Response to Jack Kevorkian," Text of Letter from General Counsel Kirk Johnson of the AMA, Oct. 10, 1995. **http://www.infinet.com/~life/euth/amaltr.htm** (Apr. 16, 1999).

Cooper, Jessia, et al. "I Question Whether You Will Ever Cease," Sentencing Statement to Dr. Jack Kevorkian, Oakland County, MI, Apr. 14, 1999. **http://www.freep.com/news/extra2/qcooper14.htm** (Apr. 16, 1999).

Humphry, Derek. "Dr. Jack Kevorkian, Prisoner #284797," Apr. 1999.

http://www.finalexit.org/dr.k.html (Apr. 16, 1999).

"Position Statement Regarding Dr. Jack Kevorkian," The Hemlock Society.

http://www.hemlock.org//common/media/position/html (Apr 16, 1999).

Samaha, Joel. *Criminal Law.* Minneapolis/St. Paul: West Publishing Company, 1996.

Sinatra, Amy. "The Kevorkian Factor," Apr. 14, 1999. **http://more.abc-news.go.com/sections/us/DailyNews/kevorkiananreax990414.html** (Apr. 16, 1999).

"The Suicide Machine: Rebecca Badger," *Detroit Free Press.* July 9, 1996.

http://www.freep.com/suicide/assisted/33.htm (Apr. 16, 1999).

Trafford, Abigail. "Dr. Death, Be Not Proud," Mar. 30, 1999.

http://newslibrary.krmediastream.com/cgi-bin/search/wp (Apr. 16, 1999).

Appendix

Web Site Bibliography

Purdue's Online Writing Lab
`http://owl.english.purdue.edu/`

Online Directory of Writing Labs
`http://www.humberc.on.ca/~coleman/cw-ref.html`

Studyweb's Grammar and Composition Site
`http://www.studyweb.com/grammar/comp/essays.htm`

The U-Vic Writer's Guide: Essay Presentation
`http://elza.lpi.ac.ru/WritersGuide/essay/proofpresent presenting.html`

Index to Composition Terms
`http://ntas-k1.sv.cc.va.us/svphilc/indexcom.htm`

Webster's Dictionary
`http://c.gp.cs.cmu.edu:5103/prog/webster`?

Bartlett's Familiar Quotations
`http://www.columbia.edu/acis/bartleby/bartlett/index.html`

Roget's Thesaurus
`gopher://odie.niaid.nih.gov/77/.thesaurus/index`

Writing Essay Exams
`http://www.wuacc.edu/services/zzcwwctr/essay-exam.wm.txt`

Revising and Editing Questions (Trinity College)
`http://www.trincoll.edu/~writcent/reveditq.html`

Narrative Essay Links

Pennsylvania State University's Narrative Hall of Fame (K. Kemmerer)

Student narrative essays

`http://www2.hn.psu.edu/Faculty/KKemmerer/narrate.html`

Using Dialogue in Composition (James Stowe)

`http://www.epcc.edu/faculty/joeo/dialog`

The Narrative Essay (Charles H. Kinzel)

`http://www.halcyon.com/mudgeon/english101p11.html`

The Pentad Taken Further (revision help)

`http://www.ccsn.nevada.edu/academics/departments/English/`
`pentad2.htm`

Explanatory Essay Links

Expository Essay

`http://www.shu.edu/academic/arts_sci/Undergraduate/english/wc/`
`expo.htm`

Expository Essays

`http://www.iss.stthomas.edu/studyguides/wrtstr3.htm`

Structuring Your Paper (Kathy Glick Miller)

`http://www.goshen.edu/~kathyjg/tutorial/struc.html`

Expository Essay

`http://www.humboldt1.com/~tyler/lessons/essays/college_`
`composition/3_expository/index.html`

Writing a Process Essay (St. Cloud State University)

`http://leo.stcloud.msus.edu/acadwrite/process.html`

Writing Cause-and-Effect Essays (Roane State Community College)

`http://www2.rscc.cc.tn.us/~jordan_jj/OWL/Cause.html`

Writing Comparison/Contrast Essays (St. Cloud State University)

`http://leo.stcloud.msus.edu/acadwrite/comparcontrast.html`

Crafting a Thesis (Steve Moiles)

`http://www.siue.edu/~smoiles/thesis.html`

Plagiarism (Princeton University)

`http://webware.princeton.edu/Writing/wc4g.htm`

Writing a Research Paper

`http://www.researchpaper.com/`

MLA Stylesheet for Electronic Sources (Janice Walker, Univ. of South Florida)

`http://www.cas.usf.edu/english/walker/mla.html`

MLA Style Documentation Guide (Capital Community-Technical College)

`http://webster.commnet.edu/mla.htm`

Using Cyber-sources (DeVry)

`http://devry-phx.edu/lrnresrc/dowsc/integrty.htm`

Surf School: An Introduction to Using the WWW

`http://www.zdnet.com/yil/filters/surfjump.html`

Kris's Research Links

`http://members.tripod.com/~kmbigalk/bigalk.html`

Links for Instructors

Hypertext and Composition (Tammy Kendig)

`http://www.lehigh.edu/~ejg1/Tammy.html`

English 101 for ESL Students (John Hitz)

`http://www.gsu.edu/~wwwesl/issue1/hitz.htm`

Teaching Composition (J. Littaue)

`http://www.bell.k12.ca.us/BellHS/Departments/English/compmenu.html`

Interpretive/Evaluative Essay Links

Literary Theory Handouts. Literary Analysis Handouts. Brigham Young University. Excellent sources for the basics of many literary theories. Also, the Literary Analysis handouts include tips for writing a literary analysis.

`http://english.byu.edu/writingctr/Handouts/indexb.htm`

Notes on Writing Film Reviews. Brigham Young University. A more involved guide to writing film reviews.

`http://english.byu.edu/writingctr/Handouts/indexb.htm`

The Writing Center Guide to Writing about Film. George Mason University. A great site that presents questions students might want to consider when writing a film review.

`http://osf1.gmu.edu/~wcenter/handouts/film.html`

A Schematic Approach to Writing about Literature and Film. George Mason University. An excellent site, complete with step-by-step, understandable directions on how to begin a literary or film review/interpretation.

`http://osf1.gmu.edu/~wcenter/handouts/wlit.html`

Basic Guidelines for Reading Literature. Laura Grossenbacher. Undergraduate Writing Center. University of Texas at Austin. An excellent guide to reading and writing about a literary work.

`http://uwc-server.fac.utexas.edu/stu/handouts/reading.html`

Writing a Thesis for a Literature Paper. Writing Techniques Handbook. University of Illinois at Urbana-Champaign.

`http://www.english.uiuc.edu/cws/wworkshop/writtechlitthesis.htm`

Writing a Literature Paper. Writing Techniques Handbook. University of Illinois at Urbana-Champaign.

`http://www.english.uiuc.edu/cws/wworkshop/writtechlitpaper.htm`

Writing about Poetry. Writing Techniques Handbook. University of Illinois at Urbana-Champaign.

`http://www.english.uiuc.edu/cws/wworkshop/writtech.poetry.htm`

Writing about Film. Writing Techniques Handbook. University of Illinois at Urbana-Champaign.

`http://www.english.uiuc.edu/cws/wworkshop/writtechfilmpaper.htm`

Handling Quotations in Papers about Literature. Writing Techniques Handbook. University of Illinois at Urbana-Champaign.

`http://www.english.uiuc.edu/cws/wworkshop/handlingquotations.htm`

Literary Tools. U-Vic Writer's Guide. A glossary of literary terms.

`http://elza.lpi.ac.ru/WritersGuide/literary/literarytermstoc.html#PoetTool`

Understanding Themes. The Literary Link for Writing and Submitting Essays. Janice Patten, San Jose State University. An excellent source for students who want to explore common themes in literature.

`http://www.sjsu.edu/faculty/patten/theme.html`

Restaurant Reviews. Northern Wisconsin Tourism, Travel, and Outdoors Reviews. A collection of well-written restaurant reviews.

`http://northernwisconsin.com/reviews.htm`

Your Movie Reviews. A site that publishes movie reviews by readers just like you!

`http://www.geocities.com/Hollywood/Academy/5218/`

Argument Essay Links

ResearchPaper.com. Infonautics. "The Web's largest collection of topics, ideas, and assistance for school-related research projects."

`http://www.researchpaper.com/`

A Guide for Writing Research Papers Based on Modern Language Association (MLA) Documentation. Humanities Department and the Arthur C. Banks, Jr., Library Capital Community-Technical College, Hartford, Connecticut.

`http://webster.commnet.edu/mla.htm.`

Janet Walker's MLA Stylesheet for Electronic Sources.

`http://www.cas.usf.edu/english/walker/mla.html`

Using Cyber-Sources. Online Writing Support Center, DeVry Institute. A very good site to help students determine whether or not a particular Web site should be used in a paper.

`http://devry-phx.edu/lrnresrc/dowsc/integrty.htm`

Quoting, Paraphrasing, and Summarizing. Purdue Online Writing Lab. Purdue University. An instructional handout.

`http://owl.english.purdue.edu/Files/31.html`

Logic in Argumentative Writing. Purdue Online Writing Lab. Purdue University. An instructional handout that covers the basics of logic and includes some exercises.

`http://owl.english.purdue.edu/Files/123.html`

Paraphrasing Exercise. Purdue Online Writing Lab. Purdue University. A great exercise to practice paraphrasing skills.

`http://owl.english.purdue.edu/Files/30E.html`

Model answers appear at: `http://owl.english.purdue.edu/Files/30A.html`

Developing an Outline. Purdue Online Writing Lab. Purdue University. Short explanation of how to write a good outline, complete with links to examples.

`http://owl.english.purdue.edu/Files/63.html`

Using Search Engines. An excellent summary of different kinds of Web search options, complete with links to different search engines.

`http://owl.english.purdue.edu/files/128.html`

WWWebster Dictionary. Merriam-Webster's 10th edition dictionary online.

`http://www.m-w.com/dictionary.htm`

How Not to Plagiarize. University of Toronto Gopher Directory. Though the Gopher form is archaic, the information is good. Check this out if you're confused about what is and what is not plagiarism.

`gopher://utl1.library.utoronto.ca/11gopher_root70:%5B_`
`services._writing_labs._plagiar%5D`

Avoiding Sexist Language. Undergraduate Writing Center. University of Texas at Austin. A short article on avoiding the "he/she" dilemma.

`http://uwc-server.fac.utexas.edu/stu/handouts/nonsex.html`

Writing an Annotated Bibliography. University of Wisconsin, Madison. An excellent site that explains the purpose and method of writing an annotated bibliography.

`http://www.wisc.edu/writing/Handbook/AnnotatedBibliography.`
`html`

Index